E-DISCOVERY

AMERICAN BAR ASSOCIATION
**Defending Liberty
Pursuing Justice**

E-DISCOVERY
TWENTY QUESTIONS AND ANSWERS

John M. Barkett

FIRST
CHAIR
·PRESS·

SECTION *of* LITIGATION
AMERICAN BAR ASSOCIATION

Cover design by ABA Publishing

Printed in the United States of America.
12 11 10 09 08   5 4 3 2 1

Library of Congress Cataloging in Publication Data

Barkett, John M.
 e-Discovery : twenty questions / John M. Barkett.
  p. cm
 Includes bibliographical references and index.
 ISBN 978-1-60442-115-6 (alk. paper)
 1. Electronic discovery (Law)—United States. I. Title.

KF8902.E42B37 2008
347.73'72—dc22   2008030725

Discounts are available for books ordered in bulk. Special consideration is given to state bars, CLE programs, and other bar-related organizations. Inquire at Book Publishing, ABA Publishing, American Bar Association, 321 N. Clark Street, Chicago, IL 60654.

www.ababooks.org

I dedicate this book to my wife, Sybil, as a partial answer to her nightly question, "*Now* what are you working on?"

CONTENTS

INTRODUCTION

E-discovery has shaken up litigation across America. Judges are dealing with e-discovery issues that were unheard of ten years ago. Arbitrators are trying to figure out e-discovery's impact in international and domestic arbitration.[1] Case law is developing in a number of areas, and conflicting decisions are not unusual. E-mail strings, backup tapes, keyword searches, production in native format, "RAM," "cache," inaccessibility—this is the jargon of "data," not "documents." Lawyers may have to associate litigation support personnel or third-party "e-discovery" vendors to generate or respond to discovery requests, or to support or contest motions for sanctions. The new world of "electronically stored information" has generated a number of questions that lawyers and judges have never had to consider or now have to consider in contexts where both large amounts of time and money may be at stake.

In this book, I synthesize the case law surrounding a number of these questions.[2] I will warn readers now that the answers are not necessarily clear in every context. Some decisions may seem irreconcilable; unique facts will make unique law. If readers take away any overall theme from this book it should be this: reasonableness should be the standard of discovery conduct for all litigants, and judges must stay engaged in the e-discovery arena to enforce Rule 1's mandate that the federal rules of civil procedure "should be construed and administered to secure the just, speedy, and inexpensive determination of every action and proceeding."

---

[1] See Barkett, *E-Discovery for Arbitrators*, 1 Dis. Res. Int. J. 129 (Dec. 2007).

[2] These questions were prompted in part by the "Electronic Discovery" class I taught at the University of Miami Law School in the fall of 2007.

CHAPTER ONE

Break Up or Stay Together? Tripping Up a Privilege Log with an E-Mail String

The opposing party has requested production of your client's documents under Fed. R. Civ. P. 34. In the process of preparing your client's privilege log under Rule 26(b)(5)(A)[1] that will accompany the document production, you come across an e-mail string containing a number of e-mails that are privileged and a number that are not. In preparing the privilege log, do you list the e-mail string as one document or do you separately itemize each document within the string that you believe is privileged, producing the nonprivileged e-mails?

In *Muro v. Target Corporation*, 2007 WL 3254463 (N.D. Ill. Nov. 2, 2007), the magistrate judge had determined that a privilege log was deficient, in part because Target had failed to itemize each e-mail in an e-mail

---

[1] The Federal Rules of Civil Procedure were "restyled" effective December 1, 2007. In some cases, rules have been renumbered. See www.uscourts.gov/rules/congress0407.htm to find the text of the new rules and supporting documentation. All cites below are to the restyled rules except, in some cases, for quotations from decisions.

string. The district court, overruling the magistrate judge, held that Rule 26(b)(5)(A) did *not* require separate itemization on a privilege log of documents contained within an e-mail string. *Id.* at *12. The district court reasoned that even when an e-mail in a string is not privileged, a second e-mail that forwards it to counsel could represent a privileged document in its entirety. The district court analogized a forwarded e-mail to a prior conversation or document that is quoted verbatim in a letter to a party's lawyer in which legal advice is sought. *Id.* The prior conversation or document may not be privileged, but what was forwarded to the lawyer would be. Thus, "[a] party can therefore legitimately withhold an entire e-mail *forwarding* prior materials to counsel, while also disclosing those prior materials themselves." *Id.* (emphasis in original). A rule that required separate itemization might result in disclosure of potentially confidential communications, the district court explained. "If the opposing party can gather enough material from the log and already produced materials to discover the topic or contents of material forwarded to counsel, then a privileged communication has been revealed to that party. Rule 26(b)(5)(A) requires only that a party provide sufficient information for an opposing party to evaluate the applicability of privilege, 'without revealing information itself privileged.'" *Id.*

The district court did not decide whether each e-mail string was privileged, however. Instead, it allowed Target to resubmit a privilege log that corrected other deficiencies in the privilege log (primarily related to the failure to identify the recipients of e-mails on "distribution lists" with respect to certain e-mails) at which point the district court would then conduct an *in camera* review of each entry on the log to evaluate the claim of privilege. *Id.* at *14–15.

The district court in *In re Universal Service Fund Telephone Billing Practices Litigation,* 232 F.R.D. 669 (D. Kan. 2005), reached a different conclusion, holding that each e-mail in a string required separate itemization. One of the parties, AT&T, argued that an e-mail string on a topic, regardless of the number of individual e-mails involved, "constitutes a single document requiring only a single privilege log entry." Citing a number of authorities, AT&T urged the magistrate judge to conclude that because an e-mail string is more akin to a "conversation" with counsel, "an e-mail strand should be treated as a single document for privilege analysis." *Id.* at 672.

The magistrate judge was not persuaded. The authorities cited by AT&T were not "directly on point" in the magistrate's view. Instead, the magistrate felt that established case law on privilege and privilege logs provided better guidance on the issue. *Id.* at 672. In addition, the magistrate said, following the approach suggested by AT&T would make Rule 26(b)(5)[2] a nullity: "[T]he obvious and unavoidable byproduct of the rule advanced by AT&T would be stealth claims of privilege which, by their very nature, could *never* be the subject of a meaningful challenge by opposing counsel or actual scrutiny by a judge." *Id.* at 672–73 (emphasis in the original).

The magistrate acknowledged that where "each and every separate e-mail within a strand is limited to a distinct and identifiable set of individuals, all of whom are clearly within the attorney-client relationship in which legal advice is being sought or given, listing the e-mail strand as one entry on the privilege log might be regarded as sufficient." *Id.* at 673. However, e-mail strings are unlike "conversations" or a "meeting with counsel," the magistrate explained, for several reasons: They may (a) span several days; (b) involve varying individuals sending, receiving, or being copied on e-mails within the strand; (c) involve some individuals "who are not part of an attorney-client relationship"; and (d) involve some e-mails that contain "entirely factual and non-privileged information" as well as e-mails that "may quite clearly seek or render legal advice." *Id.*

AT&T abandoned the claim of privilege on some e-mails after the magistrate sought more information about them. That prompted the magistrate to say that "twenty percent of the documents AT&T initially claimed as privileged would have been improperly withheld from the plaintiffs during the discovery phase of this case." Nonetheless, he elected not to find a waiver as to other withheld e-mails because this e-discovery issue was a novel one. *Id.* at 672, 674. In the future, however, despite the cost and time that would be required, the magistrate "strongly" encouraged counsel "to list each e-mail within a strand as a separate entry. Otherwise, the client may suffer a waiver of the attorney-client privilege or work product protection (and the lawyer may later draw a claim from the client)." *Id.* at 674.

However, in *United States v. ChevronTexaco Corp.*, 241 F. Supp. 2d 1065 (N.D. Cal. 2002), Chevron heeded this advice to no avail. In determining that an e-mail string was not attorney-client privileged, the district court—adopting the magistrate's recommendation—rejected Chevron's

---

[2] Fed. R. Civ. P. 26(b)(5)(A) provides: "*Information Withheld.* When a party withholds information otherwise discoverable by claiming that the information is privileged or subject to protection as trial-preparation material, the party must: (i) expressly make the claim; and (ii) describe the nature of the documents, communications, or tangible things not produced or disclosed—and do so in a manner that, without revealing information itself privileged or protected, will enable other parties to assess the claim."

decision to break an e-mail string into separate messages because each e-mail was an independent communication: "In our view, such a representation of the documents is misleading. Each e-mail/communication consists of the text of the sender's message *as well as all of the prior e-mails that are attached to it*. Therefore, Chevron's assertion that each separate e-mail stands as an independent communication is inaccurate." *Id.* at 1074 (emphasis in the original). Chevron's motivation likely is explained by this additional holding of the district court: "What is communicated with each e-mail is the text of the e-mail and all the e-mails forwarded along with it. If an e-mail with otherwise privileged attachments is sent to a third party, Chevron loses the privilege with respect to that e-mail *and all of the attached e-mails*." *Id.* (emphasis in the original).[3]

The facts usually make the law. *Muro* did not determine whether an e-mail string was privileged. It determined that a privilege log was not deficient because a party listed an e-mail string as a single document on the log. The review of the e-mail string was still to come. To the extent the last recipient was counsel and the advice being sought related to the prior e-mails in the string, the district court in *Muro* said that the privilege would attach to the e-mail string as a whole even though the nonprivileged portions of the string had to be produced separately. In the *Telephone Billing Practices* action, the magistrate was concerned at the failure by AT&T to produce nonprivileged documents that were part of what otherwise might have been, under *Muro*, a privileged e-mail string. As a result, he ordered separate itemization of the e-mails without taking into account the *Muro* court's concern that the information that was collected for counsel to obtain legal advice—a privileged communication—might be pieced together by an opposing party to discover the privileged communication. In *ChevronTexaco*, the goal of the producing party was to protect attorney-client privileged documents in an e-mail string from a waiver claim because the e-mail string had reached a third party. By itemizing each e-mail, the producing party hoped to, but did not, avoid an attorney-client privilege waiver, although it did obtain protection for the e-mails under the work-product doctrine.

Returning to the hypothetical, listing in a privilege log an e-mail string that contains attorney-client privileged e-mails is appropriate where the nonprivileged documents in the strand are produced and there has not been a waiver of the privilege because of disclosure of the e-mail string to third

---

[3] The magistrate, and thus the district court, determined, however, that the same e-mail string was protected by the work-product privilege.

parties. Even if there has been an attorney-client privilege waiver, if all of the items in the e-mail string are protected by the work-product privilege, you may be able to rely on this doctrine in listing the string as one document. In jurisdictions where there is case law on the subject, you must, of course, take into account the case law if it could dictate a different outcome. Like many aspects of e-discovery, consistency is also important across jurisdictions in litigation involving the same documents to avoid a domino effect from the loss of privilege in one jurisdiction resulting from the absence of thoughtful coordination. And it goes without saying that the "identification" requirement of Rule 26(b)(5)(A)[4] must be met in a thoughtful way.[5]

---

[4] Generally, for each document on the log, they are: the date, the author and all recipients, their capacities, a description of the subject matter, the purpose for its production, and an explanation why the document is privileged. In re Universal Service Fund Telephone Billing Practices Litigation, *supra*, 232 F.R.D. at 673 (and cases cited therein).

[5] For an in-depth discussion of the application of attorney-client privilege principles to e-mail communications and attachments, see In re Vioxx Litigation, 501 F. Supp. 2d 789 (E.D. La. 2007). Merck made a privilege claim on 30,000 documents representing 500,000 pages. A special master was appointed to establish a protocol to evaluate the claims of privilege. The special master's report is included in the opinion and was adopted in large part. This was one of the special master's protocols: "When e-mail messages were addressed to both lawyers and non-lawyers for review, comment, and approval, we concluded that the primary purpose of such communications was not to obtain legal assistance since the same was being sought from all. Neither the messages nor their attachments were found to be protected by the attorney-client privilege because, as previously noted, while the disclosure of such e-mail messages, reveals the content of what had been communicated to the lawyer (and might otherwise be privileged because the single copy sent to the attorney could have been primarily for the purpose of obtaining legal assistance), revealing this information on the face of discoverable documents (these documents would be discoverable from the files of the other recipients) breaches the confidentiality of that communication to the attorneys and thereby destroys the attorney-client privilege protection. A corporation's choices of means and format in the communications between their lawyers and employees cannot limit their adversaries' right to discovery of what otherwise is non-privileged and discoverable." *Id.* at 809. The district court was prompted to make a number of concluding remarks, including this one that mentions e-mail threads: "A primary challenge for the courts in this area is one of organization and administration. For example, it is essential that all e-mail threads be grouped together, rather than dispersed throughout several boxes of documents when produced for in camera inspection by the courts. Another challenge is created by the sheer volume of documents that must be reviewed in complex cases. The number of potentially relevant documents often reaches into the millions. It takes a legion of attorneys and paralegals to cull through the documents and recommend or decide whether each document is responsive to a request and should be produced, or whether it is instead non-responsive or privileged. In such a milieu, there is a strong bias in favor of non-production. Such circumstances also create opportunities for the attorney who concludes that delay is strategically desirable." *Id.* at 815.

CHAPTER TWO

RAM and Cache? Things You Did Not Learn in Law School

If you had to run back and forth to filing cabinets every time you worked on a file, you would not be working efficiently. Computers are designed to increase efficiency. They keep the file on your desk when you need access to it and then store it when you don't. One mechanism of temporary storage is called RAM, or "random access memory."[1] RAM keeps files being used readily available for the computer user—so you don't have to run back and forth to the file cabinet—and then erases its contents when the computer is closed down—with the files being safely stored away until they are accessed again. Does data stored fleetingly

---

[1] THE SEDONA CONFERENCE GLOSSARY: E-DISCOVERY AND DIGITAL INFORMATION (December 2007) (*Sedona Glossary*) defines RAM as follows: "Hardware inside a computer that retains memory on a short-term basis and stores information while the computer is in use. It is the 'working memory' of the computer into which the operating system, startup applications and drivers are loaded when a computer is turned on, or where a program subsequently started up is loaded, and where thereafter, these applications are executed. RAM can be read or written in any section with one instruction sequence. It helps to have more of this 'working space' installed when running advanced operating systems and applications. RAM content is erased each time a computer is turned off." www.sedonaconference.org/dltForm?did=TSCGlossary_12_07.pdf (p. 43).

in RAM constitute "electronically stored information"? Your reaction probably is, "why wouldn't it?" even as you shudder while considering whether there would ever be a duty to capture such information.

"Cache" is another temporary storage mechanism. It is defined as "a dedicated, high speed storage location which can be used for the temporary storage of frequently used data. As data may be retrieved more quickly from cache than the original storage location, cache allows applications to run more quickly. Web site contents often reside in cached storage locations on a hard drive."[2]

Two recent decisions bring RAM and cache into the e-discovery jurisprudence.

In *Columbia Pictures Industries v. Bunnell*, 2007 U.S. Dist. LEXIS 46364 (C.D. Cal. May 29, 2007), *review denied*, 245 F.R.D. 443 (C.D. Cal. Aug. 24, 2007), plaintiffs filed a copyright infringement action alleging contributory and secondary infringement, as well as inducement to infringement. Plaintiffs alleged that defendants enabled third parties, or primary infringers, to pirate copyrighted motion pictures and television shows through file links to copyrighted movies accessible through defendants' Web site. But to prove secondary infringement, plaintiffs needed to show that there were primary infringers that they could identify. *Id.* at *14. And to do that, they needed the Internet Protocol, or IP, address[3] of each person who was accessing defendants' file-sharing site. This information, the files being requested, and the date and time access was sought, were stored in "server log data" in RAM in defendants' computers. In other words, relevance was easily and persuasively shown. *Id.* at *14–15.

The magistrate judge concluded that this temporarily stored data about the users of defendants' service was still electronic information

---

[2] *Sedona Glossary*, www.sedonaconference.org/dltForm?did=TSCGlossary_12_07.pdf (p. 7).
[3] According to the *Sedona Glossary*, an IP address is "a string of four numbers separated by periods used to represent a computer on the Internet—a unique identifier for the physical location of the server containing the data." www.sedonaconference.org/dltForm?did=TSCGlossary_12_07.pdf (p. 28). The magistrate judge explained: "An IP address is a standard way of identifying a computer that is connected to the Internet. United States v. Heckenkamp, 482 F.3d 1142, 1144 (9th Cir. 2007). With an IP address, a party could identify the Internet Service Provider ('ISP') providing Internet service to the user of the computer corresponding to such IP address. See In re Charter Communications, Inc., 393 F.3d 771, 774 (8th Cir. 2005). Only the ISP, however, could link the particular IP address to an individual subscriber. *Id.* As in the case of a subscriber to a particular telephone number, the identity of the subscriber to an IP address is not necessarily indicative of the person using the service at a given time." Columbia Pictures v. Bunnell, 2007 U.S. Dist. LEXIS 46364, at *11.

and still stored. Hence, it qualified as electronically stored information under Fed. R. Civ. P. 34, irrespective of its fleeting nature. *Id.* at *21–24. Despite electronic rerouting by defendants of user requests through a third party—after plaintiffs filed their motion for sanctions—the magistrate held that the server log data was still within defendants' possession, custody, and control. *Id.* at *25–26.[4] The magistrate also rejected arguments of "undue burden" to preserve the server log data. *Id.* at *30–35.[5]

The magistrate then rejected defendants' arguments under their privacy policy, the First Amendment, the Stored Communications Act (18 U.S.C. §§ 2701–11), the Federal Wiretap Act (18 U.S.C. §§ 2510–22), and the Pen Register Statute (18 U.S.C. §§ 3121–27) and was not persuaded by arguments relating to loss of goodwill. *Id.* at *39–48.

The defendants leased their server from an Internet service provider in Amsterdam, and the lease was governed by Dutch law. So they invoked the Dutch foreign blocking statute, called the Netherlands Personal Data Protection Act, which prohibited disclosure of "information relating to an identified or identifiable person." 2007 U.S. Dist. LEXIS 46364, at *50–51. The magistrate distinguished an IP address from the identity of a person, suggesting the foreign blocking statute had no application.[6]

---

[4] After plaintiffs moved for sanctions for the failure to preserve the server log data, defendants contracted with a third party, called Panther, to receive requests for files from defendants' server. Panther's servers located in the United States serviced IP addresses of computers in the United States. Panther would route the request to defendants' server, which would respond to Panther, and then Panther would respond to the user with the requested file. Panther would cache the file so that a subsequent user requesting the same file would receive it from Panther without any contact with defendant's server. As a result, server log data was in RAM on Panther computer servers. This effort to avoid possession, custody, or control did not work. "Federal courts have consistently held that documents are deemed to be within a party's possession, custody or control for purposes of Rule 34 if the party has actual possession, custody or control, or has the legal right to obtain the documents on demand. In re Bankers Trust Co., 61 F.3d 465, 469 (6th Cir. 1995); *see also* United States v. International Union of Petroleum and Industrial Workers, AFL-CIO, 870 F.2d 1450, 1452 (9th Cir.1989) ('Control is defined as the legal right to obtain documents upon demand.'). The record reflects that defendants have the ability to manipulate at will how the Server Log Data is routed. Consequently, the court concludes that even though the Server Log Data is now routed to Panther and is temporarily stored in Panther's RAM, the data remains in defendants' possession, custody or control." 2007 U.S. Dist. LEXIS 46364, at *25–26.

[5] The magistrate accepted the expert testimony of plaintiffs that preserving the server log data involved 300 to 400 megabytes per day that could be segregated and stored cheaply. 2007 U.S. Dist. LEXIS 46364, at *32–35.

[6] "Second, even if such concerns remain, it is not clear that the Netherlands' Personal Data Protection Act applies to IP addresses, let alone to the other Server Log Data in issue, as an IP address identifies a computer, rather than a specific user of a computer. A party relying

However, even that distinction was too narrow. Relying on *Richmark Corp. v. Timber Falling Consultants*, 959 F.2d 1468, 1474–75 (9th Cir. 1992),[7] the magistrate judge held that despite a foreign statutory bar on production, discovery can be required depending upon an analysis of these factors:

the importance of the information requested in the litigation, the degree of specificity of the request, whether the information originated in the United States, the availability of alternative means of securing the information, the extent to which noncompliance would undermine important interests of the United States or compliance would undermine important interests of the state where the information is located, and the degree of hardship on the producing party and whether such hardship is self-imposed.

2007 U.S. Dist. LEXIS 46364, at *50. Applying this test, the magistrate said the server log data needed to be preserved: "The court primarily relies upon the key relevance of the Server Log Data to this action, the specificity of the data sought, the lack of alternative means to acquire such information, and the fact that defendants are United States individuals and entities who affirmatively chose to locate their server in the Netherlands at least in part to take advantage of the perceived protections afforded by that country's information security law." *Id.* at *51.

Relying on Rule 37(e),[8] the magistrate elected not to impose sanctions:

[I]n the absence of (1) prior precedent directly on point in the discovery context; (2) a specific request by [plaintiffs] to preserve Server Log Data present solely in RAM; and (3) a violation of a preservation order, this court finds that defendants' failure to retain the Server Log Data in RAM was based on a good faith belief that preservation of data temporarily stored only in RAM was not legally

---

on foreign law has the burden of showing that such law bars the discovery in issue. United States v. Vetco, 691 F.2d 1281, 1289 (9th Cir. 1981). Defendants have not met this burden." 2007 U.S. Dist. LEXIS 46364, at *49 (footnote reference omitted).

[7] The court of appeals in *Richmark* analyzed Supreme Court jurisprudence that permitted discovery despite a foreign-law prohibition on production, and relied on §442(1)(c) of the Restatement (Third) of Foreign Relations Law for the factors "that are relevant in deciding whether or not foreign statutes excuse noncompliance with discovery orders." 959 F.2d at 1474–75. The court of appeals upheld the district court's order compelling discovery by a Chinese company that was an arm of the Chinese government despite a secrecy statute of the People's Republic of China.

[8] With the December 1, 2007, amendments to the Federal Rules of Civil Procedure, former Rule 37(f) is now Rule 37(e).

required. Consequently, the court finds that evidentiary sanctions against defendants for spoliation of evidence are not appropriate.

Id. at *55. The magistrate then gave defendants seven days to begin preserving the server log data.[9]

Addressing defendants' appeal of the magistrate judge's decision, the district court agreed that data stored on RAM was discoverable electronically stored information and upheld the order of the magistrate judge. *Columbia Pictures Industries v. Bunnell*, 245 F.R.D. 443 (C.D. Cal. 2007). Because of fear that requests for data stored in RAM would create e-discovery gridlock throughout federal courtrooms in America, the district court emphasized the limited nature of the decision:

> In response to Amici's concerns over the potentially devastating impact of this decision on the record-keeping obligations of businesses and individuals, the Court notes that this decision does not impose an additional burden on any website operator or party outside of this case. It simply requires that the defendants in this case, as part of this litigation, after the issuance of a court order, and following a careful evaluation of the burden to these defendants of preserving and producing the specific information requested in light of its relevance and the lack of other available means to obtain it, begin preserving and subsequently produce a particular subset of the data in RAM under Defendants' control.

Id. at 448.

The failure to preserve data temporarily stored in cache was the focus of *Healthcare Advocates, Inc. v. Harding et al.*, 2007 U.S. Dist. LEXIS 52544 (E.D. Pa. July 20, 2007). This case involved several federal statutory claims, including a claim of copyright infringement and two common-law claims against a law firm, Harding. In connection with the defense of the litigation, Harding had viewed and printed images of archived pages of plaintiff's Web site from a Web site-archiving service using software called the Wayback Machine. At the request of the plaintiff,

---

[9] The magistrate's preservation order required defendant to "mask" or "encrypt" the identity of the user associated with an IP address and barred plaintiffs from trying to "decrypt" the user information. 2007 U.S. Dist. LEXIS 46364, at *36. The preservation order is of little import, however, because, on December 13, 2007, the district court entered a default judgment against defendants for willful spoliation of evidence, including deletion of directory headings of "torrent" files representing various television shows and deletion of a component of IP addresses. Columbia Pictures, Inc. v. Bunnell et al., 2:06-c-01093 (C.D. Cal. Dec. 13, 2007).

the archived pages were supposed to have been "blocked" by the archiving service. However, by coincidence, the archiving service's blocking function was malfunctioning on the two days the law firm looked for earlier Web pages of plaintiffs. The images were stored in cache automatically in the law firm's computers and then deleted after they were printed.[10]

Plaintiff sought sanctions for spoliation of the screenshots of its Web site that were temporarily stored in cache in the law firm computers. The district court rejected the claim.

> Ultimately, the cache files were deleted from the Harding firm's computers. However, no evidence has been presented showing that the Harding firm was responsible for erasing them. The files were deleted automatically. Plaintiff's expert, Gideon Lenkey, stated at his deposition that cache files are handled automatically by the computer. The cache files may have been emptied dozens of times before the request for production was made, which was well over three months after the Harding firm accessed the Wayback Machine.

Id. at *36. The district court also noted that the law firm provided forensic images of the computer hard drives in question, that "very little fault" could be attributed to the law firm for the loss of temporary files, and that there was no prejudice to the plaintiff because the printed copies were preserved and forensic images of the hard drives were made available allowing plaintiff's expert to "piece together what occurred." *Id.* at *37–38.[11]

Information technology managers should not panic. We have managed to justly resolve disputes in America for hundreds of years without worrying about RAM and cache. Except in the exceptional and rare case where they may become material, now would not be the time to start worrying about either.

---

[10] "A cache file is a temporary storage area where frequently accessed data can be stored for rapid access. When a computer accesses a web page, it will sometimes store a copy of the web page in its cache in case the page is needed again." 2007 U.S. Dist. LEXIS 52544, at *32.

[11] This case arose out of earlier litigation in which plaintiff had sent a letter to the law firm demanding that it preserve information associated with the archived screenshots of plaintiff's Web site. The Hardling firm complied with the request by preserving the printed images of the screenshots. The district court noted that the letter did not ask the law firm to preserve temporary cache files, prompting it to later say: "To impose a sanction on the Harding firm for not preserving temporary files that were not requested, and might have been lost the second another website was visited, does not seem to be a proper situation for an adverse spoliation inference." 2007 U.S. Dist. LEXIS 52544, at *36, *38.

CHAPTER THREE

Discovery on E-Discovery: Fishing Expedition or Smoking Gun?

E-discovery has spawned a number of cases where a requesting party is suspicious about the thoroughness of a production of electronically stored information. Requesting parties believe that the "smoking gun" lies in an electronic file somewhere in corporate computer-storage media. Producing parties are quick to label as a "fishing expedition" any effort to question the bona fides of an electronic production. Generally speaking, the closer to a fishing expedition discovery on discovery is, the less likely it is to be allowed. Similarly, the closer it is to finding a smoking gun, the more likely it will be allowed.

A number of cases make the point. The district court in *In re Ford Motor Company*, 345 F. 3d 1315 (11th Cir. 2003), a personal injury action, ordered Ford to give the plaintiff, Russell, access to Ford's Master Owner Relations Systems I, II, and III (MORS) and Common Quality Indicator System (CQIS) databases.[1] The district court made no findings that Ford had

---

[1] Plaintiff had sought access to conduct searches for claims related to inertial unlatching of the RCF-67 seatbelt buckle, the basis of plaintiff's claim. "MORS records all customer contacts with Ford, and CQIS records contacts by dealers, personnel, and other sources." 345 F.3d at 1316.

"failed to comply properly with discovery requests." *Id.* at 1316. Ford successfully petitioned the court of appeals to vacate the order.[2] Ford argued that it had done a search and produced relevant, nonprivileged materials; that plaintiff did not identify any discovery abuse by Ford; and that the discovery rules did not permit unfettered access to the databases in any event. *Id.* The court of appeals agreed with Ford and vacated the district court's order: "While some kind of direct access might be permissible in certain cases, this case has not been shown to be one of those cases. Russell is unentitled to this kind of discovery without—at the outset—a factual finding of some non-compliance with discovery rules by Ford. By granting the sweeping order in this case, especially without such a finding, the district court clearly abused its discretion." *Id.* at 1317.[3] *See also Balfour Beatty Rail, Inc. v. Vaccarello,* 2007 U.S. Dist. LEXIS 3581, at *7–8 (M.D. Fla. Jan. 18, 2007) (following *Ford,* disallowing access to defendants' hard drives where plaintiff made no showing to justify access).

In *Scotts Co., LLC v. Liberty Mutual Insurance Co.,* 2007 WL 1723509 (S.D. Ohio June 12, 2007), plaintiff demanded a forensic search of defendant's computer systems, network servers, and databases and demanded the production of backup tapes of certain information systems. The magistrate judge first explained that the 2006 amendments to Fed. R. Civ. P. 34 "simply clarify that discovery of electronically stored information stands on equal footing with discovery of paper documents." *Id.* at 5 (citing Fed. R. Civ. P. 34 Advisory Committee's Note on 2006 Amendments). Without a justification, therefore, the magistrate said, "plaintiff is no more entitled to access to defendant's electronic information storage

---

[2] The writ was styled as one for mandamus or prohibition. The court of appeals relied on the Advisory Committee Notes to Rule 34(a) in granting the writ. Those notes explain that where data "can be made usable by the discovering party only through respondent's devices, respondent may be required to use his devices to translate the data into usable form. In many instances, this means that respondent will have to supply a print-out of computer data." 345 F.3d at 1316 (quoting Fed. R. Civ. P. 34(a) Advisory Committee Note (1970 amend.). However, Rule 34(a) "does not give the requesting party the right to conduct the actual search. While at times—perhaps due to improper conduct on the part of the responding party—the requesting party may need to check the data compilation, the district court must 'protect respondent with respect to preservation of his records, confidentiality of nondiscoverable matters, and costs.'" *Id.* (quoting from the Advisory Committee Note).

[3] The court of appeals added that the district court "did not discuss its view of Ford's objections and provided no substantive explanation" for its ruling. *Id.* at 1316. On the merits, the district court also "established no protocols for the search" and did not "even designate search terms to restrict the search." *Id.* at 1317.

systems than to defendant's warehouses storing paper documents." *Id.* Plaintiff's request was based on the "mere suspicion" that defendant may be withholding discoverable information. "Plaintiff's speculation" was not a sufficient basis upon which to grant the request, the magistrate held. *Id.* at *6.[4] *See also Hubbard v. Potter, 2008 WL 43867,* *4 (D.D.C. Jan. 3, 2008) (explaining that Rule 26(g) requires a certification of the correctness of a discovery response, so that where some electronic records were produced, plaintiffs' speculation that more electronic information existed was insufficient to permit discovery on e-discovery: "I cannot find on this record that the theoretical possibility that other electronic documents might exist justifies the additional discovery plaintiffs seek").[5]

A plaintiff's insistence that only its expert would properly search mirror images of hard drives from defendant's computers did not persuade a magistrate judge to allow such access. In *Calyon v. Mizuho Securities USA, Inc.,* 2007 U.S. Dist. LEXIS 36961 (S.D.N.Y. May 18, 2007), plaintiff

---

[4] In 2007 U.S. Dist. LEXIS 43005, at *6–7, the decision contains a helpful list of other decisions where parties have sought discovery-on-e-discovery, including Playboy Enters., 60 F. Supp. 2d 1050, 1054 (S.D. Cal. 1999) ("allowing access to party's computer system on a finding of systematic deletion of relevant e-mails after litigation had commenced"); Williams v. Mass. Mut. Life Ins. Co., 226 F.R.D. 144, 146 (D. Mass. 2005) ("denying motion to appoint computer forensic expert because moving party failed to present any 'credible evidence that Defendants are unwilling to produce computer-generated documents'"); Bethea v. Comcast, 218 F.R.D. 328, 329–30 (D.D.C. 2003) ("denying motion to compel because, '[i]n the context of computer systems and computer records, inspection or seizure is not permitted unless the moving party can demonstrate that the documents they seek to compel do, in fact, exist and are being unlawfully withheld'"); Simon Prop. Group L.P. v. Simon, Inc., 194 F.R.D. 639, 641 (S.D. Ind. 2000) ("allowing plaintiff to inspect defendant's computer system because plaintiff demonstrated 'troubling discrepancies with respect to defendant's document production'"); Balboa Threadworks, Inc. v. Stucky, 2006 U.S. Dist. LEXIS 29265, 2006 WL 763668, at *4 (D. Kan. Mar. 24, 2006) ("permitting imaging of defendants' computer where defendants' representation that no responsive materials existed on computer was contradicted by their production of e-mail created on that computer").

[5] *Cf. United States v. O'Keefe et al.,* 2008 U.S. Dist. LEXIS 12220 (D.D.C. Feb. 12, 2008). This is a criminal matter where the district court judge ordered the government to search for exculpatory evidence. Defendants claimed that the government's electronic production was deficient. The magistrate judge said that accusations that the government destroyed or failed to produce documents ordered to be produced "are serious." "I must therefore remind the defendants of the wise advice given the revolutionary: 'If you strike at a king, kill him.' If the defendants intend to charge the government with destroying information that they were obliged to preserve and produce pursuant to Judge Friedman's order or the due process clause itself, they must make that claim directly and support it with an evidentiary basis—not merely surmise that they should have gotten more than they did. If they do not do so within 21 business days of this opinion, I will deem any such claim to have been waived." Id. at *20–21.

alleged that its former employees stole proprietary information. Plaintiff and the new employer, Mizuho, had agreed to create mirror images of the former employees' computer hard drives. The only issue was over who could forensically examine them. Plaintiff sought an order allowing its forensic expert to search the mirror images to find evidence of the heist. Plaintiff asserted, without specific support, that only its expert had the incentive to perform a diligent search.

Apart from raising privacy concerns for unfettered access to these hard drives, defendants responded by telling the magistrate that their forensic expert would work "cooperatively" with Calyon's counsel and expert "on an on-going basis to develop and refine search techniques to ensure that all responsive information is identified." They also acknowledged that their expert would search for information "located in the hard drives' hidden areas." *Id.* at *17–18.

The magistrate judge surveyed recent discovery-on-discovery cases where imaging and inspection of hard drives had been addressed. *Id.* at *9–11. The magistrate observed that the outcomes in these cases had been based on a balancing of relevance, need, and justification for the search, and—where such discovery was allowed—protocols to protect privilege and privacy concerns. The magistrate further observed that Calyon was not arguing that defendants failed to produce all responsive documents that had been requested or that there were any discrepancies or inconsistencies in their responses to prior discovery requests. Calyon also did not argue that any documents or data had been lost and did not identify specific information it was seeking to recover from the mirror images. *Id.* at *16–17. Calyon's only basis for the discovery it sought was the incentive its expert would have to find the allegedly stolen proprietary information. That was not enough for the magistrate: "Calyon's argument about proper incentives was simply too generalized a basis for granting it *carte blanche* access to the individual defendants' personal hard drives, access that Calyon itself acknowledges as 'extraordinary.'" *Id.* at *18.

As the magistrate in *Calyon* recognized, access to opponents' hard drives has been justified in certain circumstances. In *Ameriwood Indus., Inc., v. Liberman*, 2006 U.S. Dist. LEXIS 93380, *7–8 (E.D. Mo. Dec. 27, 2006), the district court was persuaded that mirror images of defendants' hard drives fell into the category of "not reasonably accessible" due to undue burden and cost under Rule 26. *Id.* at *11–12. However, an e-mail from a defendant to a third party suggested that defendants had violated a noncompete clause. The e-mail was obtained by the plaintiff from the third party and had not been produced by the defendants. *Id.* at *11.

In light of that fact, the nature of the case, and plaintiff's willingness to bear the cost, the district court found good cause to order a forensic search of defendants' hard drives. *Id.* at *16. The district court's order established the following protocol for the production:

1. Plaintiff's forensics expert had to execute a confidentiality agreement;
2. Computers would be imaged at defendant's place of business;
3. Plaintiff's expert would provide the parties with a report describing the equipment produced (by name, model, serial number, name of hard drive and model and serial number, and name of network card manufacturer and model and serial number) and the expert's actions with respect to each piece of equipment;
4. Plaintiff's expert would recover all available word-processing documents, incoming and outgoing e-mail messages, presentations, spreadsheets, and other files including "deleted" files;
5. Recovered documents would be provided to defendants' counsel; and
6. Defendants' counsel had twenty days to review the records for privilege and responsiveness and to update its response to plaintiff's request for production, including creation of a privilege log.[6]

Id. at *16–20. The district court determined that this procedure and an appropriate protective order would sufficiently address defendants' privacy concerns. *Id.* at *15.[7] *See also Orrell v. Motorcarparts of America, Inc.*, 2007 U.S. Dist. LEXIS 89524, *23 (W.D.N.C. Dec. 4, 2007) (ordering, at requesting party's expense, forensic examination of producing party's home computer where producing party and her husband had given conflicting testimony about the information that had been contained on the

---

[6] This protocol was adopted by the district court in Cenveo Corp. v. Slater et al., 2007 U.S. Dist. LEXIS 8281, at *5–10 (E.D. Pa. Jan. 31, 2007), another case involving former employees accused of misappropriating trade secrets to divert business away from plaintiff. It appears from the opinion that the defendants' only objection to the request for imaging and forensic examination of defendants' computers was based on a fear of disclosure of privileged information. *Id.* at *2–3.

[7] The district court later granted default judgment in favor of plaintiffs as a sanction for defendants' spoliation of evidence. Ameriwood, 2007 U.S. Dist. LEXIS 74886 (E.D. Mo. July 3, 2007). Information had been erased from defendants' hard drives after the order for forensic examination issued, but before the examination took place. *Id.* at *10. The district court entered default judgment after finding defendants' explanations for the erasure "ranging from the improbable to the impossible." *Id.* at *18.

home computer before it allegedly "crashed" and where producing party had her laptop "wiped" using "Evidence Eliminator" software before she returned it to defendant-employer after she was terminated).

Peskoff v. Faber, 2007 244 F.R.D. 54 (D.D.C. 2007) took a slightly different approach. The issue was missing e-mails between Peskoff and Faber. Peskoff testified about his persistent use of e-mail to communicate with Faber and at least one e-mail between them existed. The search conducted by Faber did not result in the production of any e-mails that Peskoff received or authored between mid-2001 and mid-2003, and there was no explanation why this gap existed, where these e-mails might currently be located, or what steps were taken to locate the e-mails. These, among other considerations, convinced the magistrate judge that it was appropriate "to ascertain the cost of forensic testing of the computers and server at issue to see if it justifies a forensic search of them." *Id.* at *63.[8] The magistrate then ordered counsel to collaborate with the magistrate "on what can be described as a request for proposals seeking bids from qualified forensic computer technicians to perform an examination of all the computers that were owned by NextPoint in the period of Peskoff's employment and of the network server used by NextPoint during the same period to ascertain whether" there existed e-mails sent to and received by Peskoff in that period and any e-mails in which the word "Peskoff" appears anywhere in the e-mail. *Id.* The bid was also to include the "cost to convert the found e-mails into another readable format such as TIFF or PDF." Once the bids were received, the magistrate said the parties could then "brief whether any of the proposals received should be accepted and, if so, who shall bear the cost of doing the search." *Id.*[9]

---

[8] Where deposition testimony reveals that an electronic search was inadequate, a producing party can expect that more will be demanded of it. *Atmel Corp. v. Authentec Inc.*, 2008 U.S. Dist. LEXIS 10850 (N.D. Cal. Jan. 31, 2008) (where a Rule 30(b)(6) corporate designee witness testified that he did not know whether the e-mail files of the plaintiff's chief executive officer and the e-mail accounts of nine other persons who worked in the product area in question had been searched, plaintiff was ordered to search these accounts and to provide declarations from persons "most knowledgeable affiliated with Plaintiff's company, not outside counsel, detailing the search done for these documents." *Id.* at *7.

[9] The magistrate assumed that "bidders will respond to the request for proposals without cost in the hopes of ultimately securing the business. If I am wrong in that assumption, the parties should advise me and counsel and I will have to convene to ascertain what to do." He also ordered "counsel for the parties to initially draft a request for proposals and then appear before me to begin the process of seeking bids." 2007 WL 2416119, at *11. In fact, bids were received and the low bid was $33,000. *Peskoff v. Faber*, 2008 WL 2649506 (D.D.C. July 7, 2008). The magistrate judge then held a cost-shifting hearing following which the magistrate determined that the producing party should pay 100 percent of the costs of the

Williams v. Massachusetts Mut. Life Ins. Co., et al., 226 F.R.D. 144 (D. Mass. 2005) rejected a request for "discovery on discovery" but ordered preservation of the electronic records in question. Plaintiff claimed that defendant Massachusetts Mutual had possession of an e-mail reflecting that the defendant engaged in discriminatory practices. Massachusetts Mutual denied the existence of the e-mail and, following its own forensic analysis, proffered an e-mail that, it believed, was the e-mail to which plaintiff was referring (and contained no suggestion that the defendant engaged in discriminatory practices). Plaintiff sought access to Massachusetts Mutual's data storage systems to search for himself and offered to pay the costs of doing so. The district court refused this access, explaining: "Before permitting such an intrusion into an opposing party's information system—particularly where, as here, that party has undertaken its own search and forensic analysis and has sworn to its accuracy—the inquiring party must present at least some reliable information that the opposing party's representations are misleading or substantively inaccurate." *Id.* at 146 (citations omitted). The district court, however, ordered Massachusetts Mutual to preserve electronic records searched in response to plaintiff's motion: "The court, however, will order Defendants to preserve all documents, hard drives and e-mail boxes which were searched by their forensic expert in response to Plaintiff's motion. Such an order, in the court's estimation, is not unduly burdensome and is necessary, at a minimum, to preserve Plaintiff's appellate rights." *Id.* at 146–47 (record citation omitted). *See also Palgut v. City of Colorado Springs*, 2007 WL 4277564, at *3 (D. Colo. Dec. 3, 2007) (following *Williams* and *Scotts* in holding that plaintiff did not satisfy the burden of proof to justify appointment of a computer forensic expert to examine the city's computer system).

In the paper world, a discarded document leaves no trail. In the digital world, when a document is deleted, it may still exist. But unless there is a good reason to doubt the bona fides of a search for electronically stored information by a producing party, discovery on e-discovery should not be permitted.

---

forensic examination because the information sought was relevant and not duplicative, and because of his failure to preserve relevant backup tapes and suspend auto-delete tools, conduct searches previously suggested by the magistrate, and explain these failings. *Id.* at *3–4.

CHAPTER FOUR

Must a Party Preserve Backup Tapes?

Judge Scheindlin's proclamations in *Zubulake v. UBS Warburg LLC*, 220 F.R.D. 212 (S.D.N.Y. 2003) (*Zubulake IV*) continue to resonate throughout the federal district courts.

> Must a corporation, upon recognizing the threat of litigation, preserve every shred of paper, every e-mail or electronic document, and every backup tape? The answer is clearly, "no". Such a rule would cripple large corporations, like UBS, that are almost always involved in litigation. As a general rule, then, a party need not preserve all backup tapes even when it reasonably anticipates litigation.

Id. at 217. The exception, however, makes the rule:

> The scope of a party's preservation obligation can be described as follows: Once a party reasonably anticipates litigation, it must suspend its routine document retention/destruction policy and put in place a "litigation hold" to ensure the preservation of relevant documents. As a general rule, that litigation hold does not apply to inaccessible backup tapes (e.g., those typically maintained solely for the purpose of disaster recovery), which may continue to be recycled on the schedule set forth in the company's policy. On the other hand, if backup tapes are accessible (i.e., actively used for

information retrieval), then such tapes would likely be subject to the litigation hold.

However, it does make sense to create one exception to this general rule. If a company can identify where particular employee documents are stored on backup tapes, then the tapes storing the documents of "key players" to the existing or threatened litigation should be preserved if the information contained on those tapes is not otherwise available. This exception applies to all backup tapes.

Id. at 218. The "general rule" has been cited approvingly a number of times: *Columbia Pictures Industries v. Bunnell*, 2007 U.S. Dist. LEXIS, at *55 (C.D. Cal. May 29, 2007), *review denied*, 245 F.R.D. 443 (C.D. Cal. 2007); *Consol. Aluminum Corp. v. Alcoa, Inc.*, 2006 U.S. Dist. LEXIS 66642, at *8, n.4 (M.D. La. July 19, 2006).

Oxford House, Inc. v. City of Topeka, 2007 U.S. Dist. LEXIS 31731 (D. Kan. Apr. 27, 2007), also invoked the general rule from *Zubulake IV* with respect to a demand by the requesting party to obtain e-mails on backup tapes. Defendant received a demand letter from plaintiff on August 12, 2005. The e-mails in question had been deleted in June 2005. While the e-mails went to backup tapes, the backup tapes were rotated every six weeks. More than six weeks had passed between June 2005 and August 12, 2005. Hence there were no responsive e-mails on backup tapes. Plaintiff's motion to compel was thus denied because the defendant had fully responded to plaintiff's request for production.

It was the magistrate's alternative holding that resulted in the citation to *Zubulake IV*:

When parties put a litigation hold policy on destruction of documents in response to pending litigation, "that litigation hold does not apply to inaccessible back-up tapes (e.g., those typically maintained solely for the purpose of disaster recovery), which may continue to be recycled on the schedule set forth in the company's policy." The record in this case indicates that the back-up tapes are used for disaster recovery purposes. Therefore, it is the court's view that defendant had no duty prior to August 12, 2005, to retain or recover the deleted electronic messages.

Id. at *12 (footnotes omitted). Of course, if there was no duty to preserve prior to August 12, it does not matter how backup tapes were used by the defendant. And if the backup tapes existed after August 12, when the duty to preserve arose, the exception in *Zubulake IV* presumably would have applied since the city knew that the tapes were the only storage media containing the e-mails in question. Nonetheless, the case cautiously falls into the "general rule" camp.

In *Cache La Poudre Feeds, LLC v. Land O'Lakes, Inc. et al.*, 2007 U.S. Dist. LEXIS 15277 (D. Colo. Mar. 2, 2007), plaintiff argued that defendant had a duty to safeguard backup tapes from recycling. The magistrate did not read defendant's duty quite as broadly:

> As noted, counsel for Land O'Lakes was required to undertake a reasonable investigation to identify and preserve relevant materials in the course of responding to Plaintiff's discovery requests. Such an investigation would not automatically include information maintained on computer back-up tapes. "As a general rule, [a] litigation hold does not apply to inaccessible back-up tapes...which may continue to be recycled on the schedule set forth in the company's policy." *Zubulake v. UBS Warburg LLC*, 229 F.R.D. at 431. As of December 2006, a party responding to discovery requests must identify but need not produce electronically stored information that is not reasonably accessible because of undue burden or cost. One such source of information might be back-up tapes containing archived data.

Id. at *48–49 (footnote and citation omitted). The magistrate later held that a party "must ensure that relevant information is retained on a continuing basis once the preservation obligation arises," but did not address the application of this principle to backup tapes because what was at issue was a practice of wiping clean the hard drives on computers of former employee/key players after the duty to preserve arose. *Id.* at *31–32. The clear sense one gets from reading the opinion is that had relevant information existed only on backup tapes, this magistrate judge would have faulted the defendant for failing to preserve the backup tapes, i.e., the exception in *Zubulake IV* would have been endorsed.[1]

Not every court necessarily reads *Zubulake IV* the same way. The court in *AAB Joint Venture v. United States*, 2007 U.S. Claims LEXIS 56 (Ct. Cl. Feb. 28, 2007) cited *Zubulake IV* for the proposition that "the scope of the duty to preserve extends to electronic documents, such as e-mails and back-up tapes." *Id.* at **26.[2]

---

[1] *Cf.* E*Trade Sec. LLC v. Deutsche Bank AG, 230 F.R.D. 582, 592 (D. Minn. 2005) ("Because NSI [a defendant] relied on its backup tapes to preserve evidence that was not preserved through a litigation hold, NSI should have retained a copy of relevant backup tapes because it was the sole source of relevant evidence").

[2] The court cited to 220 F.R.D. at 216, where Judge Scheindlin wrote: "In this case, the duty to preserve evidence arose, at the latest, on August 16, 2001, when Zubulake filed

Toussie v. County of Suffolk, 2007 WL 4565160 (S.D.N.Y. Dec. 21, 2007) invoked *Zubulake IV*'s articulation of the duty to preserve backup tapes related to key players. The magistrate judge had ordered the county to do a search at its expense of its backup servers for responsive e-mails because only two e-mails had been produced from active data. *Id.* at *1. An outside vendor restored 417 backup tapes resulting in production of over 2,000 pages of e-mails and attachments. Plaintiffs sought an adverse inference instruction as a sanction, in part because the county had not discontinued a practice of overwriting backup tapes after the litigation was initiated in 2001. *Id.* at *5. This was significant because post-complaint e-mails were relevant and the county had failed to implement a litigation hold after the complaint was filed, meaning that the e-mails were potentially only available on backup tapes. Finding that the duty to preserve had been violated, the magistrate was critical of the county for using backup tapes, in effect, as its filing system: "To begin with, the county did not alter its document and retention procedures in any way as a result of the lawsuit. While the evidence gleaned from the county's IT professional was somewhat confusing, what clearly emerged from the testimony was that even after the lawsuit was filed, the county continued to save electronic data in a virtually inaccessible format." *Id.* at *6. In determining that the county had the "culpable state of mind" needed to justify imposition of an adverse inference instruction, the magistrate judge held that the failure to implement a litigation hold was grossly negligent and the failure to preserve all potentially relevant backup tapes was negligent. *Id.* at *8. It was in explaining the difference between the two that the magistrate, referring again to the discussion of the scope of the duty to preserve in *Zubulake IV*, said: "Although the law is now clear that any back up tapes containing the documents of a key player must be preserved and accessible, *see id.*, the law with respect to back up tapes was not clear in 2001. *Zubulake*, 220 F.R.D. at 220 (whether duty to preserve extends to back up tapes has been grey area)." *Id.* at *8. Where a litigation hold is not implemented in a timely manner and e-mails generated after a duty to preserve arises are relevant, under *Toussie*, using backup media as a filing system for the e-mails of key players will result

---

her EEOC charge. At that time, UBS's in-house attorneys cautioned employees to retain all documents, including e-mails and backup tapes, that could potentially be relevant to the litigation." There was no reference in *AAB Joint Venture* to Judge Scheindlin's later discussion of the general rule and the exception to the general rule.

in a duty both to preserve and restore the backup media to retrieve responsive e-mails.[3]

Zubulake IV was also the focal point in *Treppel v. Biovail Corp.*, 2008 WL 866594 (S.D.N.Y. Apr. 2, 2008). The duty to preserve arose on May 1, 2003, when Biovail learned of the lawsuit. *Id.* at *5. Biovail implemented an ineffective litigation hold in May 2003 and preserved one backup tape in December 2003 following receipt of a preservation letter from plaintiff. *Id.* at *5–6.[4] Plaintiff sought an adverse inference instruction as a sanction for Biovail's failure to preserve relevant electronically stored information. *Id.* at *5. In holding that the duty to preserve had been violated, the magistrate judge faulted Biovail for failing to preserve backup tapes from a key time period: "This failure is most troubling with regard to the failure to preserve the monthly backup tapes that existed when litigation commenced in May 2003. Since Biovail's policy is to retain its monthly backups for one year before overwriting them, as of May 1, 2003, it presumably possessed backups dating back to May 2002, the month in which many of the underlying events at issue in this action ensued. That backup, however, was subsequently overwritten and destroyed." *Id.* at *6. Invoking *Zubulake IV* for the proposition that not all backup tapes have to be preserved, the magistrate said it was "equally clear" that "Biovail should have retained the monthly backup tapes of the relevant servers from the previous year, since these were quite likely to contain files that were later deleted."[5]

---

[3] Ultimately, the magistrate rejected the requested sanction. While 9 percent of the backup tapes were unavailable and users may have deleted e-mails because of the failure to implement a litigation hold, plaintiffs were unable to show there was a reason "to believe that any of those e-mails would have provided any additional support of plaintiffs' claims." 2007 WL 4565160 at *9. Instead, plaintiffs were awarded their costs of bringing their motion and of participation in numerous hearings before the magistrate on the county's production of e-mails. *Id.* at *10.

[4] One of the key players was Melnyk, the CEO of Biovail. He used a laptop. His laptop was not backed up for preservation purposes until August 2005, which was significant because Melnyk's e-mails were downloaded directly to his laptop and were not preserved on Biovail's e-mail servers. In other words, any e-mails deleted by Melnyk were not preserved elsewhere. 2008 WL 866594 at *3.

[5] On the issue of culpability, the magistrate then cited *Toussie* in holding that the failure to preserve backup tapes in May 2003 was "merely" negligent because the duty to preserve backup tapes was a grey area in 2003. 2008 WL 866594 at *8. However, the failure to preserve relevant backup tapes after the plaintiff's preservation demand letter was received was regarded by the magistrate as "gross negligence" because *Zubulake IV* had been decided by then. *Id.* Ultimately, an adverse inference instruction was rejected because, as was the case in *Toussie*, plaintiff could not show prejudice from Biovail's breach of the duty to

In most cases, the subject of backup tapes is not going to arise, and litigants can safely continue to recycle backup tapes. Under this case law, where litigants know that accessible data presents an incomplete production picture with respect to relevant documents, litigants need to figure out relatively quickly the time period for potentially relevant electronically stored information, where the data of key players reside, and the backup tape recycling schedule.

---

preserve: "Mr. Treppel relies on generalized assertions such as that 'it is highly improbable that relevant documents regarding Treppel were not created between December 2002 and December 2003' and that the defendants' failure to suspend overwriting of e-mail backups 'almost certainly resulted in spoliation of significant relevant evidence.' Such assertions are insufficient to establish relevance." *Id.* at *10. Biovail was ordered to search certain backup tapes, and plaintiff was permitted to conduct a forensic examination of the Melnyk's laptop at Biovail's expense. As for costs, the magistrate held: "If it becomes necessary to undertake additional discovery that the plaintiff would not otherwise have conducted to obtain the equivalent of any destroyed evidence, the plaintiff may make an application for costs at that time." *Id.* at *11.

CHAPTER FIVE

Downgrading Data to Inaccessible Format: Risky Business?

As more electronic storage information systems become the subject of case law, there is a growing body of law on the conversion of accessible data into inaccessible data, or "data downgrades." Two magistrate judges from the same court have expressed opposite views on the subject: In *Treppel v. Biovail Corp.*, 233 F.R.D. 363 (S.D.N.Y. Feb. 6, 2006), the magistrate judge held: "[P]ermitting the downgrading of data to a less accessible form—which systematically hinders future discovery by making the discovery more costly and burdensome—is a violation of the preservation obligation." Contrast this holding with *Quinby v. WestLB AG*, 2005 U.S. Dist. LEXIS 35583 (S.D.N.Y. Dec. 15, 2005), where the magistrate held that there is no duty to keep data in an accessible format. "I decline to sanction defendant for converting data from an accessible to inaccessible format, even if they should have anticipated litigation." *Id.* at *27, n.10.

Rule 34(a)(1)(A)[1] is the starting point to understand the debate. Under Rule 34(a)(1)(A), the requesting party can serve on a producing party a request within the scope of Rule 26(b):

---

[1] Rule 34(a)(1) was formerly numbered as Rule 34(a) and has been restyled.

(1) to produce and permit the requesting party or its representative to inspect, copy, test, or sample the following items in the responding party's possession, custody, or control:

(A) any designated documents or electronically stored information—including writings, drawings, graphs, charts, photographs, sound recordings, images, and other data or data compilations—stored in any medium from which information can be obtained either directly or, if necessary, after translation by the responding party into a reasonably usable form;...

The Advisory Committee Note to Rule 34(b) attempts to flesh out a producing party's obligations under Rule 34(a). The Advisory Committee recognized that there may be situations where the producing party would have to "translate information" for a requesting party:

Rule 34(a) requires that, if necessary, a responding party "translate" information it produces into a "reasonably usable" form. Under some circumstances, the responding party may need to provide some reasonable amount of technical support, information on application software, or other reasonable assistance to enable the requesting party to produce electronically stored information in the form in which it is ordinarily maintained, as long as it is produced in a reasonably usable form.[2]

The Advisory Committee may have had in mind a case like *Sattar v. Motorola, Inc.*, 138 F.3d 1164 (7th Cir. 1998). In *Sattar*, the court of appeals found reasonable the district court's decision requiring downloading of data from four-inch tapes to conventional computer disks or a computer hard drive, loaning Sattar a copy of the necessary software, or offering Sattar on-site access to Motorola's computer system to review 210,000 pages of e-mail that Sattar otherwise lacked the equipment and software to read. *Id.* at 1171.

So far so good. What does the Advisory Committee say about "data downgrades"? This is the pertinent excerpt from the Note to Rule 34(b):

But the option to produce in a reasonably usable form does not mean that a responding party is free to convert electronically stored information from the form in which it is ordinarily maintained to a different form that makes it more difficult or burdensome for the requesting party to use the information efficiently in the litigation.

---

[2] www.uscourts.gov/rules/supct1105/Excerpt_CV_Report.pdf (p. 67).

> If the responding party ordinarily maintains the information it is producing in a way that makes it searchable by electronic means, the information should not be produced in a form that removes or significantly degrades this feature.[3]

What is not accounted for in this quote is the duty to preserve. If a duty to preserve does not exist, what an entity does with its data as part of a records management system should not matter. Hence, for example, e-mail can be moved to backup on a schedule that makes the e-mail less accessible or inaccessible without running afoul of the "reasonably usable form" language of Rule 34(a)(1)(A). After that point, and after litigation exists or a duty to preserve otherwise exists, Rule 26(b)(2)(B)[4] then kicks in: the producing party may claim that the e-mails are not reasonably accessible because of undue burden or cost, and, if the producing party is successful in meeting this burden, the requesting party, if it elects to pursue the matter, must show good cause. Courts then will conduct a marginal utility analysis. Courts will likely evaluate the reasonableness of the records management protocol that resulted in the "data downgrade" and decide whether to order production with or without conditions, like the shifting of some or all of the costs of production to the requesting party.

If a duty to preserve is found to have attached and, using this same example, e-mails were automatically moved to backup tapes after the duty arose, a court might call this a "data downgrade," require production under the "translation" requirement of Rule 34(a), and never get to cost-shifting under Rule 26(b)(2)(B).[5]

---

[3] *Id.*

[4] Rule 26(b)(2)(B) provides: "A party need not provide discovery of electronically stored information from sources that the party identifies as not reasonably accessible because of undue burden or cost. On motion to compel discovery or for a protective order, the party from whom discovery is sought must show that the information is not reasonably accessible because of undue burden or cost. If that showing is made, the court may nonetheless order discovery from such sources if the requesting party shows good cause, considering the limitations of Rule 26(b)(2)(C). The court may specify conditions for the discovery." The text of Rule 26(b)(2)C) appears in n. 13.

[5] "Conditions for the discovery" under Rule 26(b)(20)(B) might involve cost-shifting. See, e.g., Haka v. Lincoln County, 2007 U.S. Dist. LEXIS 64480 (W.D. Wis. Aug. 29, 2007) (limiting search of external hard drives initially to e-mails only, ordering requesting party to tailor search term requests "to the narrowest set with which he is comfortable," and requiring the parties to split the costs 50 percent each); Pipefitters Local No. 636 v. Mercer Human Resource Consulting, Inc., 2007 U.S. Dist. LEXIS 52169 (E.D. Mich. July 19, 2007) (district court granted motion to strike magistrate's order requiring requesting party to pay 100 percent of the costs of restoring electronic data where a Rule 26(b)(2)(B) analysis had not been undertaken by the magistrate judge).

The issue will be addressed usually in the context of a request for cost-shifting.[6] In *Quinby v. WestLB*, the magistrate saw nothing wrong with a decision to search only backup tapes for responsive information because the accessible records management systems in place would not have produced all of the responsive data:

> Thus, because the back-up tapes contain the most complete source of e-mails—covering all the relevant e-mail accounts and most, if not all, of the time periods for which plaintiff seeks e-mails—and the alternative sources only cover a narrow time frame, a limited number of users and the data on these sources can be incomplete, it was logical for defendants to consider the back-up tapes to be the primary source for the production of the e-mails.

2005 U.S. Dist. LEXIS 35583, at *25. The magistrate did not have as positive a view of the producing party's request for cost-shifting. "Assuming for the purposes of the sanctions motion that defendant's cost-shifting motion is granted, defendant will likely have only a portion of the fees shifted to plaintiff." *Id.* at *28, n.11.

The magistrate subsequently evaluated the cost-shifting claim. *Quinby v. WestLB*, 2006 U.S. Dist. LEXIS 64531 (S.D.N.Y. Sept. 5, 2006). The

---

[6] Or, if the backup tapes were not kept and a duty to preserve had attached, the issue might come up in the context of a motion for sanctions. *Cf.* Broccoli v. Echostar Comm. Corp. et al., 229 F.R.D. 506 (D. Md. 2005) where the district court issued an adverse inference instruction as a result of a failure to preserve documents. The district court first explained the defendant's e-mail retention protocol: "Under Echostar's extraordinary e-mail/document retention policy, the e-mail system automatically sends all items in a user's 'sent items' folder over seven days old to the user's 'deleted items' folder, and all items in a user's 'deleted items' folder over 14 days old are then automatically purged from the user's 'deleted items' folder. The user's purged e-mails are not recorded or stored in any back up files. Thus, when 21-day-old e-mails are purged, they are forever unretrievable. The electronic files, including the contents of all folders, sub-folders, and all e-mail folders, of former employees are also completely deleted 30 days after the employee leaves Echostar. Again, under normal circumstances, such a policy may be a risky but arguably defensible business practice undeserving of sanctions." *Id.* at 510. But here the protocol was not material because the district court found that a duty to preserve came into existence before the e-mails in question could have been destroyed even under this protocol and, after reviewing deposition testimony, then concluded: "In short, the evidence of a regular policy at Echostar of 'deep-sixing' nettlesome documents and records (and of management's efforts to avoid their creation in the first instance) is overwhelming." *Id.* at 511. Many companies do not regard e-mail as a "business record," so Echostar's protocol is not necessarily "extraordinary" or "risky," but when a duty to preserve exists, whatever the protocol, it must be suspended, or other steps must be taken, to ensure that relevant documents in existence at the time the duty arises are preserved.

magistrate bounded the analysis by reference to the timing of the data conversion in relation to a duty to preserve:

> I submit, however, that if a party creates its own burden or expense by converting into an inaccessible format data that it should have reasonably foreseen would be discoverable material at a time when it should have anticipated litigation, then it should not be entitled to shift the costs of restoring and searching the data....
>
> If, on the other hand, it is not reasonably foreseeable that the particular evidence in issue will have to be produced, the responding party who converts the evidence into an inaccessible format after the duty to preserve evidence arose may still seek to shift the costs associated with restoring and searching for relevant evidence.

Id. at *29–30. There were a number of custodians whose e-mails were in issue. The magistrate decided that the defendant should have anticipated that the e-mail of all of these custodians but one, Barron, would have been sought in discovery in likely litigation. So the cost-shifting analysis was conducted only with respect to the e-mails of Barron. The magistrate ultimately shifted to the plaintiff 30 percent of the costs of production as to Barron's e-mails. *Id* at *52. Because the backup tapes at issue contained e-mails of the other custodians (which the defendant had to produce at its sole expense), and not just Barron's, the magistrate prorated the costs of restoration. The requesting party ultimately was required to pay $447.89. *Quinby v. WestLB AG*, 2007 U.S. Dist. LEXIS 2955, *3–4 (S.D.N.Y. Jan. 4, 2007).

In *In re Veeco Instruments, Inc. Securities Litigation*, 2007 U.S. Dist. LEXIS 23926 (S.D.N.Y. Apr. 2, 2007), the setting was similar; e-mails did not exist anywhere but on backup tapes. However, the parties could not agree on an electronic discovery protocol. Plaintiff sought e-mail from the backup tapes for a specified time period for specified individuals. Defendant resisted the request. There was no discussion of when the duty to preserve attached. The magistrate judge found good cause to require the production in part because the e-mails did not exist anywhere else:

> E-mails sent or received by Defendants relating to the issues herein could constitute important relevant evidence and are reasonably calculated to lead to admissible evidence. It has not been demonstrated that said information is reasonably available from any other easily accessed source. The discovery requests are specific. The resources of the parties are not an issue. Accordingly, the

Court directs that the Defendant restore the backup tapes for the time period from August 2004 through March 2005 to produce the requested non-privileged documents.

Id. at *5. The magistrate deferred the cost-shifting determination until after production, which was estimated to cost something considerably less than $124,000 (an original estimate before plaintiff tailored the discovery request): "The Court directs that Defendant shall produce the electronic discovery set forth herein initially at its own expense. Defendant shall prepare an affidavit detailing the results of its search, as well as the time and money spent. The court will then conduct the appropriate cost-shifting analysis." *Id.* at *7.

In *AAB Joint Venture v. United States*, 2007 U.S. Claims LEXIS 56 (Ct. Cl. Feb. 28, 2007), the trial court found that the defendant United States was under a duty to preserve e-mails as of July 2002. Since that date e-mails had been transferred to backup tapes. The trial court held that the decision to transfer the e-mails to backup tapes "does not exempt Defendant from its responsibility to produce relevant e-mails." *Id.* at **33. The trial court ordered the United States initially to restore one-fourth of the backup tapes at its expense.[7]

In reaching its conclusion, the trial court in *AAB Joint Venture* relied on *In re Brand Name Prescription Drug Litigation*, 1995 WL 360526 (N.D. Ill. 1995) and *Linnen v. Wyeth*, 1999 WL 462015, 10 Mass L. Rprt. 189 (Mass. Super Ct. June 16, 1999). In *Prescription Drug*, the issue was payment of $50,000 to $70,000 by CIBA (a defendant) or the plaintiffs to recover e-mail from backup tapes. In evaluating "undue burden," the district court recognized the equities on each side: "On the one hand, it seems unfair to force a party to bear the lofty expense attendant to creating a special computer program for extracting data responsive to a discovery request. On the other hand, if a party chooses an electronic storage method, the necessity for a retrieval program or method is an ordinary and foreseeable risk." *Id.* at *2. Ultimately, the district court required the producing party to pay the cost of producing the e-mail: "Class Plaintiffs should not be forced to bear a burden caused by CIBA's choice of electronic storage." *Id.* The district court did, however, order the plaintiffs to

---

[7] Defendant had estimated the cost to restore the tapes at between $85,000 and $150,000. The trial court settled on restoration of 25 percent of the tapes initially to evaluate the relevance of the information retrieved. "The parties will then have an opportunity to argue before the Court whether or not additional restoration of back-up tapes is likely to lead to production of relevant evidence and consequently who should bear the cost for additional restoration." 2007 U.S. Claims LEXIS 56, at **36.

narrow their request in an attempt to bring the costs down. *Id.* at *3. There was no discussion of when the duty to preserve arose and, of course, the decision predates the e-discovery rules by more than a decade. Without expressing any views on the outcome, one would think that the analysis today would be different.

In *Linnen*, the issue again was recovery of e-mail from backup tapes. The requesting party sought fees and costs associated with its motion to compel. The trial court ordered Wyeth to bear the costs and fees associated with the e-mail discovery, including the depositions of two individuals and the requesting party's costs and fees associated with pursuing the motion. The trial court relied on *Prescription Drug* in holding that the cost of restoring e-mail from backup tapes should be borne by Wyeth: "[T]his is one of the risks taken on by companies which have made the decision to avail themselves of the computer technology now available to the business world. To permit a corporation such as Wyeth to reap the business benefits of such technology and simultaneously use that technology as a shield in litigation would lead to incongruous and unfair results." 1999 WL 462015, at *6 (citation omitted). The trial court, however, also said it would look for ways to minimize the ultimate costs of restoration to the extent possible and deferred ordering production until a sampling of backup tapes for relevant documents was completed in an associated multidistrict litigation. *Id.* The case is colored also by the fact that the tapes in question were not produced until after a large number of depositions had already been taken and after initial denials that any stored tapes existed. The conversion of data in relation to a duty to preserve also was not in issue.[8] Again without expressing any views on the outcome, the analysis today under the federal rules would be very different than the one undertaken here.

Aubuchon Co., et al. v. BeneFirst, LLC, 2007 U.S. Dist. LEXIS 44574 (D. Mass. Feb. 6, 2007), did not involve backup tapes and also did not focus on the date the duty to preserve attached. Instead, it involved a database that was extremely difficult to search, so much so that it caused the magistrate judge to speculate why:

---

[8] The duty to preserve was indirectly implicated in the analysis because there was a separate motion for sanctions with respect to certain backup tapes that were not retained by Wyeth. The trial court had issued a preservation order, and Wyeth failed to suspend recycling of backup tapes after the order was issued. "The recycling, and resultant destruction, of those back-up tapes was in clear violation of the court's order." 1999 WL 462015, at *10. The trial court required the defendant to pay the costs associated with the motion and reserved ruling on a "spoliation inference" instruction until the time of trial. *Id.* at *13.

However, because of BeneFirst's method of storage and lack of an indexing system, it will be extremely costly to retrieve the requested data. I am hard pressed to understand the rationale behind having a system that is only searchable by year of processing, then claims examiner, then the month of processing, and finally the claims date. None of these search criteria reflect the name of the individual claimant, the date that the claimant received the medical service, who the provider was, or even the company that employed the benefit holder. It would seem that such a system would only serve to discourage audits and the type of inquiries that have led to the instant litigation.

Id. at *11–12. Nonetheless, the magistrate conducted a cost-shifting factor analysis resulting in an order to the defendant to retrieve the information requested by the plaintiff at the defendant's sole expense. *Id.* at *18–19.[9] One has to think that the reasonableness of defendant's records management system affected the magistrate's thinking, even though it was not mentioned in the analysis of cost-shifting factors.

Static Control Components, Inc. v. Lexmark International, Inc., 2006 WL 897218 (E.D. Ky. Apr. 5, 2006), also involved accessible information that was difficult to search. Electronically stored information was sought from a pre-November 2004 database that was maintained in a form that was not text-searchable and was run on software modified for defendant's use. The software was no longer commercially available. *Id.* at *3. Defendant had, however, offered to make the database available at its facility where information could be printed and then reviewed by defendant's counsel for privilege, which would not be waived as part of the defendant's proposal. Plaintiff had instead demanded a backup of

---

[9] *Cf.* Zurich American Ins. Co. v. Ace American Reinsurance Co., 2006 WL 3771090 (S.D.N.Y. Dec. 22, 2006). An affiant attested that Ace processed thousands of claims and its computer system was incapable of segregating claims by the amount of the claim, the type of claim, the identity of the "cedent" (in this case, that would be Zurich or other insurance companies who "ceded" an insurance obligation to the reinsurer), or the reason the claim may have been denied. Magistrate Judge Francis was not sympathetic: "A sophisticated reinsurer that operates a multimillion dollar business is entitled to little sympathy for utilizing an opaque data storage system, particularly when, by the nature of its business, it can reasonably anticipate frequent litigation." But the magistrate recognized that the volume of data accumulated by Ace made a search of its entire database "infeasible," so he ordered the parties to propose a protocol for sampling Ace's claim files "to obtain examples of claims files in which issues of the allocation of policy limits has been addressed." He also permitted Zurich's counsel to take the deposition of the affiant and other persons familiar with Ace's data storage system. If Ace objected to Zurich's sampling proposal, "it shall support its objections with specific evidence of the cost and burden involved." *Id.* at *2.

the database, saying it would extract what data it wanted. It characterized defendant's access proposal as "meaningless":

> In reply, SCC counters that the above-referenced plan is unacceptable for several reasons, but chiefly because Lexmark represents that "the only way to retrieve information from this database is by inputting a specific caller's name, phone number, or call reference number (which is an internal designation created by Lexmark.)" SCC points out that it does not have these names and numbers it would need to obtain any information from this database; therefore, "review" of this information on Lexmark's terms would be fruitless, since it would be unable to gain *meaningful access* to the data.

Id. at 3 (record citation omitted; emphasis in the original).

The magistrate judge ordered Lexmark to produce the database in a reasonably usable form, but did apply the "outside counsel only" provision of a protective order governing discovery in the matter:

> The Magistrate Judge concludes that Lexmark is obligated to produce its pre-November 2004 database of this information to SCC in a reasonably usable form for SCC. *See* 8A Wright & Miller, *Federal Practice and Procedure*, § 2218 (2d ed. 1994). The Federal Rules do not permit Lexmark to hide behind its peculiar computer system as an excuse for not producing this information to SCC. *See Dunn v. Midwestern Indemnity*, 88 F.R.D. 191, 197 (S.D. Ohio 1980); *Kozlowski v. Sears, Roebuck & Co.*, 73 F.R.D. 73, 75 (D. Mass. 1976). Thus, SCC's motion to compel the production of the database predating November 2004 will be granted; however, since that portion of the database predating November 2004 is proprietary to Lexmark, the Magistrate Judge also concludes that it should be categorized as "Outside Counsel Only" information and produced under the terms of the Protective Order governing discovery in this case.

Id. at *4.[10] Once relevance was established, defendant did not appear to leave the magistrate much of a choice when defendant argued that

---

[10] In May 2007, the United States Advisory Committee on the Federal Rules of Evidence proposed a new Rule 502 that would protect the privilege and preclude waiver claims by third parties if production is made to an opponent in litigation under a "quick peek" or "clawback" agreement as long as there is a court order providing such protection. See www.uscourts.gov/rules/Reports/EV05-2007.pdf. On February 27, 2008, S.2450, which adopts Rule 502, was passed in the Senate and was referred to the House Committee on the Judiciary. See www.govtrack.us/congress/bill.xpd?bill=s110-2450.

"production of relevant records from Lexmark's database prior to November 2004 in hard copy format was not reasonably possible." *Id.* at *3.

The e-discovery rules' amendments went into effect eight months after this decision was rendered. Had they been applicable, the magistrate presumably would have evaluated a claim of "undue burden or cost" by the producing party and a request for cost-shifting and a response of good cause by the requesting party. But this was less a case of production in a "reasonably usable form" and more of one of production of the database because the database was not text searchable, the software was no longer commercially available, the software had been modified for defendant's use, and production in hard copy format was not "reasonably possible." The citations to *Kozlowski*[11] and *Dunn*[12] seem out of place

---

[11] Kozlowski v. Sears, Roebuck & Co., 73 F.R.D. 73 (D. Mass. 1976) was a product-liability action involving pajamas that allegedly ignited and severely burned the plaintiff. Plaintiff sought all documents of similar complaints from Sears that the district court determined was discoverable. For many years, Sears had indexed complaints alphabetically by name of claimant rather than by type of product. Sears claimed there was no practical way to determine whether similar complaints had been made other than by reviewing all of the entries in the index. Sears called that an "impossible task." Sears was required, however, the district court held, to show why discoverable documents should not be produced. Compliance that would be costly or time-consuming "is not ordinarily sufficient reason to grant a protective order where the requested material is relevant and necessary to the discovery of evidence." *Id.* at 76. Because the requested documents were within the scope of Rule 26, the plaintiff had a demonstrable need for the documents and no other access to them, production was ordered. *Id.* The district court added, and presumably this is why the magistrate in *Static Control* cited the case: "The defendant seeks to absolve itself of this responsibility by alleging the herculean effort which would be necessary to locate the documents. The defendant may not excuse itself from compliance with Rule 34, Fed. R. Civ. P., by utilizing a system of record-keeping which conceals rather than discloses relevant records, or makes it unduly difficult to identify or locate them, thus rendering the production of the documents an excessively burdensome and costly expedition. To allow a defendant whose business generates massive records to frustrate discovery by creating an inadequate filing system, and then claiming undue burden, would defeat the purposes of the discovery rules." *Id.* (citations omitted). The outcome of the case is colored by the facts that the plaintiff was indigent and Sears never bothered to ask the manufacturer of the product about similar complaints, even though Sears was being indemnified by the manufacturer and Sears had access to the documents under the indemnity. *Id.* at 76–77. Had the index been kept in electronic form, and had Sears made a claim that the information was "not reasonably accessible because of undue burden or cost," the result would have been the same under a good cause/cost-shifting analysis. See, e.g., Aubuchon Co., et al. v. BeneFirst, LLC, discussed above, which also involved a difficult-to-search index and where the producing party was required to respond at its sole cost.

[12] Dunn v. Midwestern Indemnity, et al., 88 F.R.D. 191, 197 (S.D. Ohio 1980) involved a claim by plaintiffs that they were denied homeowner's insurance because they were black.

here in that the magistrate ordered the database produced to the plaintiff rather than ordering the defendant to search the database.

Disability Rights Council of Greater Washington v. Washington Met. Transit Auth., 242 F.R.D. 139 (D.D.C. 2007) involved resistance by a litigant to the restoration of backup tapes where the litigant had failed to retain e-mails after a duty to preserve arose and the data resided only on backup tapes. The magistrate was unsympathetic to the producing party's plea for protection:

> While the newly amended Federal Rules of Civil Procedure initially relieve a party from producing electronically stored information that is not reasonably accessible because of undue burden and cost, I am anything but certain that I should permit a party who has failed to preserve accessible information without cause to then complain about the inaccessibility of the only electronically stored information that remains. It reminds me too much of Leo Kosten's definition of chutzpah: "that quality enshrined in a man who, having killed his mother and his father, throws himself on the mercy of the court because he is an orphan."

Id. at *26 (citation omitted). Nonetheless, the magistrate here, too, engaged in a good-cause determination under Rule 26(b)(2)(C)[13] and found good

---

Plaintiffs sought "minute information" about defendants' computer capabilities, including information about their computer equipment, raw data, programs, and data management systems, and wanted production of "tapes which contain information about past and present policyholders in the Dayton, Ohio area. In some cases, the information is sought for a specified time period; in others, no time limits are indicated." *Id.* at 193. The district court determined first that the request was appropriate under Rule 26 in part because denial of coverage to other black applicants might show a pattern of refusing to insure black homeowners in black neighborhoods. *Id.* at 197. Each of the insurance companies argued that the costs, manpower, and feasibility of compliance created an undue burden. The district court decided to hold an evidentiary hearing to determine whether "compliance with said requests is merely time-consuming and laborious, or whether it is impossible. The Court wishes to stress that impracticability is not to be equated with impossibility in this context. Other issues to be addressed at the proposed hearing concern what, if any, time constraints should be imposed on plaintiffs' requests which contain no time limits, and whether there is merit to plaintiffs' claim that they need certain information, dating back to January 1, 1970, in order to adequately evaluate trends and experience." After citing *Kozlowski*, the district court added that it would not "be receptive to defendants' impossibility contentions insofar as they are grounded in the peculiar manner in which defendants maintain their computer systems." *Id.* at 198.

[13] Rule 26(b)(2)(C) provides: "On motion or on its own, the court must limit the frequency or extent of discovery otherwise allowed by these rules or by local rule if it determines that: (i) the discovery sought is unreasonably cumulative or duplicative, or can be obtained

cause to require the defendant to produce information on backup tapes in part because the e-mails existed only on backup:

> As to factors one through four, the request is for the e-mails of specific persons, and there is absolutely no other source from which the electronically stored information can be secured, thanks to WMATA's failure to impose a litigation hold.

Id. at *29.

Courts do not run businesses. Companies can be expected to make data storage decisions based on business needs. A company that needs to manage tens of millions of pages of documents will direct an information technology department to do so cost-effectively in a manner that will support operations. A profit maximizer sets up databases to support business growth and profits without regard to what a hypothetical requesting party may seek in unanticipated future litigation. However, courts *do* run discovery. Thus, the importance of properly painting a producing party's data storage and retrieval picture for a court cannot be underestimated. In addition, because data disappears with auto-recycling programs, litigants must pay attention to the duty to preserve, especially in a prelitigation setting where the trigger of the duty can be the subject of debate. The relationship of the duty to preserve to the conversion of data to a less accessible format, and the length of time that backup tapes are kept even before a duty to preserve arises,[14] will continue to create a tension between records management practices and electronically stored information that is "reasonably usable" under Rule 34(a)(1)(A) and information that is "not reasonably accessible" under Rule 26(b)(2)(B).

---

from some other source that is more convenient, less burdensome, or less expensive; (ii) the party seeking discovery has had ample opportunity to obtain the information by discovery in the action; or (iii) the burden or expense of the proposed discovery outweighs its likely benefit, considering the needs of the case, the amount in controversy, the parties' resources, the importance of the issues at stake in the action, and the importance of the discovery in resolving the issues."

[14] See, e.g., Oxford House, Inc. v. City of Topeka, 2007 U.S. Dist. LEXIS 31731 (D. Kan. Apr. 27, 2007), discussed above, where backup tapes were kept for six weeks but a demand letter was sent after the tapes for the time period in issue had already been recycled.

CHAPTER SIX

Vendor, Vendor, on the Wall, Who's the Fairest of Them All?

Vendors can cause a client e-discovery headaches. Where they have done so, courts have not been particularly forgiving of the client or its lawyers.

PSEG Power New York Inc. v. Alberici Constructors, 2007 U.S. Dist. LEXIS 66767 (N.D.N.Y. Sept. 7, 2007), involved the separation of 3,000 e-mails from their attachments. The magistrate judge described the vendor's problem:

> The separation of the e-mails from the attachments happened at the interface between the different software used by PSEG and the vendor when reducing the documents in a form that could be reviewed by counsel. *Id.* It appears that the "vendor's software was not compatible with the HTML format in which PSEG had provided its documents and that this incompatibility had resulted in the parent child link between the e-mails and attachments being broken." Upon discovering this dilemma, the parties immediately engaged in a dialogue to determine if a reasonable solution to this technological snafu was feasible. Much to our chagrin, remarrying the e-mails to their attachments will be formidable and costly.

Id. at *7 (record citation omitted). The magistrate later elaborated. The e-mails and their attachments were "inadvertently divorced because of the incompatibility of PSEG's internal computer software and its vendor's software as they attempted to put all of these downloaded documents into a reviewable and searchable format."

However, no data was lost. The e-mails and the attachments could be remarried. The issue was who would pay the cost. *Id.* at *14. The magistrate called the problem a "discovery quagmire created by PSEG's vendor." *Id.* at *25. In the end, it placed the cost of remarrying the attachments with the e-mails on PSEG, giving PSEG the choice of doing so in hard copy or electronically. *Id.* at *34–35.

In re Seroquel Products Liability Litigation, 2007 U.S. Dist. LEXIS 61287 (M.D. Fla. Aug. 21, 2007), involved vendor mistakes with load files and metadata. E-mails were also separated from their attachments. Blaming the vendor did not save the producing party from imposition of a sanction. The magistrate judge cited Sedona Principle 6.d: "Ultimate responsibility for ensuring the preservation, collection, processing, and production of electronically stored information rests with the party and its counsel, not with the nonparty consultant or vendor."[1] That says it all.[2]

---

[1] BEST PRACTICES RECOMMENDATIONS & PRINCIPLES FOR ADDRESSING ELECTRONIC DOCUMENT PRODUCTION (June 2007). The document can be downloaded by going to the Sedona Conference Web site. See www.thesedonaconference.org/dltForm?did=TSC_PRINCP_2nd_ed_607.pdf. The Sedona Conference Working Group on Electronic Document Retention and Production is the author of this publication. The Sedona Conference working group series "is a series of think-tanks consisting of leading jurists, lawyers, experts and consultants brought together by a desire to address various 'tipping point' issues in each area under consideration." www.thesedonaconference.org/.

[2] Well, maybe not all. Sullivan & Cromwell (s&c) sued a vendor for alleged mistakes in handling e-discovery issues. In a complaint filed December 28, 2007, in the Southern District of New York, S&C accused Electronic Evidence Discovery, Inc. (EED), of "untimely and inaccurate" work. S&C asked the district court to declare that it did not have to pay a $710,000 bill from EED. See www.law.com/jsp/article.jsp?id=1199441137204. EED responded by suing S&C in King County Superior Court in Washington on January 7, 2008, demanding payment of $660,016.17, plus interest in the amount of $58,592.07. The matter was quickly and confidentially settled according to a January 18, 2008, report in the NEW YORK LAW JOURNAL.

CHAPTER SEVEN

The Sanctions Hit Parade: Caveat Advocatus?

E-discovery is focusing attention on the myriad sanctions provisions in the federal rules. Some sanctions provisions are mandatory, and some are discretionary. Consider these cases.

Rule 16(f)

Rule 16(f)(1) authorizes a district judge to issue "any just orders," including those authorized by Rule 37(b)(2)(A)(ii)–(vii),[1] if a party or its lawyer: "(A) fails to appear at a scheduling or other pretrial conference; (B) is substantially unprepared to participate—or does not participate in good faith—in the conference; or (C) fails to obey a scheduling or other pretrial order." There is a mandatory component to Rule 16(f) as well regarding attorneys' fees. Rule 16(f)(2) provides:

> Instead of or in addition to any other sanction, the court must order the party, its attorney, or both to pay the reasonable expenses—including attorney's fees—incurred because of any noncompliance with this rule, unless the noncompliance was substantially justified or other circumstances make an award of expenses unjust.

Tracinda Corp. v. DaimlerChrysler AG, et al., 502 F.3d 212 (3rd Cir. 2007), was not an e-discovery case, but it warrants the close attention of e-discovery

---

[1] See n. 7, *infra*.

practitioners. The case involved the discovery by defendant during trial of previously unproduced handwritten notes of a witness. The notes were immediately produced after they were found, but the failure to produce the notes during discovery violated the Rule 16 pretrial order requiring parties to comply with discovery requests for relevant information. The district court temporarily adjourned the trial, appointed a special master to find out why the notes were not produced earlier (the nonproduction was inadvertent), and required two witnesses to be recalled. Plaintiff, which lost the case on the merits, sought $1.1 million in sanctions for its costs to address the delayed production, but unilaterally agreed to accept $556,061. The district court accepted the proposition. The Third Circuit affirmed because the production was late and prejudicial and caused these costs to be incurred. It was not sympathetic to defendant's policy arguments:

> DaimlerChrysler argues to the contrary that our holding will open the door to a "flood of satellite litigation" over Rule 16(f) expenses every time a document production error is unearthed after the close of discovery, which can be a common occurrence in complex litigations. DaimlerChrysler points out that scheduling orders often require document production to be completed before depositions commence, at which time witnesses often identify relevant documents not previously produced.
>
> We do not concur with this assessment of the results of our decision. Production errors discovered at the pre-trial stage of litigation will result in little, if any, expense or prejudice to the opposing party and therefore are not likely to warrant the imposition of sanctions under Rule 16(f). On the other hand, if a litigant knows that even inadvertent failure to produce relevant documents may result in a sanction when the existence of the documents is discovered during trial, the litigant may exercise more care in ensuring that all relevant documents are produced.

Id. at 243.

Electronic document production is fraught with the potential for inadvertent failures to produce. It will not be a surprise to see this language quoted in an e-discovery case before too long.

Rule 26(g)

Under Rule 26(g)(1)(A), disclosures pursuant to Rule 26(a)(1) must be signed by an attorney of record. That signature represents a certification with respect to a disclosure "that to the best of" the signer's "knowledge, information, and belief, formed after a reasonable inquiry," the disclosure "is complete and correct as of the time it is made." Under Rule 26(g)(3), if "without substantial justification," the certification is made in violation of Rule 26(g), the district court "upon motion or on its own, *must impose* an appropriate sanction on the signer, the party on whose behalf the signer was acting, or both. The sanction may include an order to pay the reasonable expenses, including attorney's fees, caused by the violation." (Emphasis added.)

In *Cache La Poudre Feeds, LLC v. Land O'Lakes, Inc. et al.*, 2007 U.S. Dist. LEXIS 15277 (D. Colo. Mar. 2, 2007), defendant producing party continued to expunge electronically stored information on hard drives of computers of former employees after the duty to preserve attached. Defendant's in-house counsel did not independently verify that a litigation hold was being followed. He assumed that the former employees' e-mails were located on shared drives of current employees, but this also was never verified. This misfeasance prompted the district court to say: "Under the circumstances and without some showing of a reasonable inquiry, it is difficult to understand how Defendants' retained counsel could legitimately claim on July 7, 2005 that Land O'Lakes had 'made every effort to produce all documentation and provide all relevant information.'" *Id.* at 55. Citing the Advisory Committee Note to Rule 26(g) on the obligation of counsel affirmatively to engage in pretrial discovery in a responsible manner consistent with the spirit and purposes of Rules 26 through 37,[2] and the mandatory sanction language of Rule 26(g), the district court sanctioned the defendant.[3] *Id.* at *56–57, 80. But because there was no substantial prejudice by the failure to implement and monitor an

---

[2] The magistrate recognized that a lawyer is entitled to rely on the assertions of the client under Rule 26(g) provided that "'the investigation undertaken by the attorney *and the conclusions drawn therefrom* are reasonable under the circumstances.' Advisory Committee Notes to the 1983 Amendments to Fed. R. Civ. P. 26(g). *But [see] also* Metropolitan Opera Ass'n, Inc. v. Local 100 Hotel Employees and Restaurant Employees International Union, 212 F.R.D. 178, 221–24 (S.D.N.Y. 2003) (holding that defense counsel failed to comply with Rule 26(g) by, *inter alia,* never adequately instructing defendant as to its overall discovery obligations, by failing to inquire about the client's document storage procedures and capabilities, by failing to implement a systematic procedure for document production or retention, and by failing to ask important witnesses for documents), *adhered to on reconsideration,* 2004 U.S. Dist. LEXIS 17093, 2004 WL 1943099." 2007 U.S. Dist. LEXIS 15277, at *40–41.

[3] The magistrate held that a litigation hold, "without more, will not suffice to satisfy the 'reasonable inquiry' requirement in Rule 26(g)[(1)]. Counsel retains an on-going responsibility to take appropriate measures to ensure that the client has provided all available information and documents which are responsive to discovery requests." *Id.* at *56–57 (citation omitted).

adequate preservation program and because plaintiff did not succeed on other aspects of its motion to compel and motion for sanctions, the district court awarded plaintiff $5,000 plus the costs of a court reporter and the transcription for one deposition. *Id.* at *81.

Rule 26(g) sanctions reached Middle Earth in Peter Jackson's now-resolved fight with New Line Cinema over his share of profits from the *Lord of the Rings* movies. In *Wingnut Films Ltd. v. Katja Motion Pictures Corp., et al.*, 2007 U.S. Dist. LEXIS 72953 (C.D. Cal. Sept. 18, 2007), New Line Cinema committed a number of discovery sins, including failures to search, failures to produce documents, and misrepresentations to the district court. With respect to e-discovery sought by the plaintiff, New Line failed to search for documents on New Line's e-mail and document servers, individual desktop or laptop computers, "or otherwise." *Id.* at *34–35. Some employees were asked to collect e-mails, but they were given "little or no guidance" on what to retrieve. *Id.* at *36. New Line also failed to suspend its document retention program for electronically stored information.[4]

The magistrate explained that Rule 26(g) requires that "counsel make a reasonable investigation and effort to certify that the client has provided all information and documents available to it which are responsive to a discovery request—something that New Line's counsel has plainly failed to do here." *Id.* at *54–55. There was no substantial justification for the failure; hence Rule 26(g) sanctions were mandated. *Id.* at *55.[5]

The magistrate required that New Line retain an outside vendor jointly selected by the parties to search all servers, desktops, and laptops related to key players for electronically stored information using agreed-upon keyword search terms. The vendor was required to create a log of every document located. No documents identified by the vendor could be withheld from production by New Line Cinema because of relevance. New Line had to pay all costs of the vendor. If the parties could not agree on any aspect of the document search protocol, the dispute was to be "promptly submitted" to the magistrate for resolution. *Id.* at *51. The magistrate also gave defendants an opportunity to "file any additional Opposition as to why a reasonable, substantial portion of Wingnut

---

[4] Every employee's e-mail inbox was purged every thirty days, and backup tapes "are wiped clean on a weekly basis." Backup tapes for other electronic documents, such as word-processing files, were recycled after one year. 2007 U.S. Dist. LEXIS 72953, at *37.

[5] The magistrate held that sanctions were also awardable under Rule 37(b)(2) for failure to comply in a timely fashion with discovery orders. *Id.* at *54.

attorneys' fees and costs in the appropriate amount of $125,000 should not be imposed as sanctions on defendants." The opposition had to be limited to the issue of the amount of fees, not the entitlement to fees. *Id.* at *57. Depositions of fact witnesses regarding the failure to suspend document retention policies and documents lost as a result of this failure, the magistrate intimated, would be permitted after documents were produced under the magistrate's order. *Id.*[6]

Rule 37(b)(2)(A)

Rule 37(b)(2)(A) states that a court "*may*" issue "just orders" against a party that "fails to obey an order to provide or permit discovery." A number of sanctions are then provided for the district court's consideration.[7]

Rule 37(b)(2) was cited by the magistrate judge as an alternative basis to award sanctions in *Wingnut Films Ltd. v. Katja Motion Pictures Corp., supra.*

> Rule 37(b)(2) provides that, in addition to the other sanctions the court may in its discretion impose, "the court shall require the party failing to obey [an] order or the attorney advising that party or both to pay the reasonable expenses, including attorney's fees, caused by the failure." Fed. R. Civ. P. 37(b)(2). Except where the offender's conduct was "substantially justified" or an award of expenses is otherwise "unjust"—neither of which describes the present case—

---

[6] *See also* E*Trade Sec. LLC v. Deutsche Bank AG, 2005 U.S. Dist. LEXIS 3021, at *29–36 (D. Minn. Feb. 17, 2005) (magistrate judge found a violation by counsel of Rule 26(g)(1)'s certification obligations and ordered each of two defendants to pay $5,000 for costs incurred "because of the violation").

[7] The order granting sanctions must be "just." Rule 37(b)(2)(A) provides in full: "If a party or a party's officer, director, or managing agent—or a witness designated under Rule 30(b)(6) or 31(a)(4)—fails to obey an order to provide or permit discovery, including an order under Rule 26(f), 35, or 37(a), the court where the action is pending may issue further just orders. They may include the following: (i) directing that the matters embraced in the order or other designated facts be taken as established for purposes of the action, as the prevailing party claims; (ii) prohibiting the disobedient party from supporting or opposing designated claims or defenses, or from introducing designated matters in evidence; (iii) striking pleadings in whole or in part; (iv) staying further proceedings until the order is obeyed; (v) dismissing the action or proceeding in whole or in part; (vi) rendering a default judgment against the disobedient party; or (vii) treating as contempt of court the failure to obey any order except an order to submit to a physical or mental examination." Rule 37(b)(2)(C) adds: "Instead of or in addition to the orders above, the court must order the disobedient party, the attorney advising that party, or both to pay the reasonable expenses, including attorney's fees, caused by the failure, unless the failure was substantially justified or other circumstances make an award of expenses unjust."

Rule 37 sanctions are mandatory and "must be applied diligently both 'to penalize those whose conduct may be deemed to warrant such a sanction, [and] to deter those who might be tempted to such conduct in the absence of such a deterrent.'" *National Hockey League v. Metropolitan Hockey Club, Inc.*, 427 U.S. 639, 643, 96 S. Ct. 2778, 49 L. Ed. 2d 747 (1976) (*per curiam*).

2007 U.S. Dist. LEXIS 72953, at *54.

Rule 37(b)(2) was also cited by the magistrate judge in *In re Seroquel Products Liability Litigation*, 2007 U.S. Dist. LEXIS 61287 (M.D. Fla. Aug. 21, 2007). This case involved a number of discovery failings recited in the opinion:

- A keyword search was inadequate;
- Attachments to e-mails were not provided;
- Relevant e-mails were omitted;
- The de-duplication method used was "mysterious";
- Production was tardy and purposefully sluggish;
- Efforts to prevent and solve technical problems were "woefully deficient"; and
- There was a failure to foster consultation between the two sides' technical staffs.

Id. at *39–40, *41.

Ultimately, the magistrate judge held that the producing party had been "purposefully sluggish" and uncooperative in its e-document production:

AZ has not been as cooperative as possible in resolving the custodial issues. It is undisputed that the production "completed" on June 30, 2007 had load file, metadata, page break and key word search problems, making the 10 million pages of documents unaccessible, unsearchable, and unusable as contemplated under the Rules. It was not clear at the July 26 hearing, or even as of the date of this Order, that these profound technical issues have been resolved by the re-production efforts delivered to Plaintiffs on July 20, 2007. The Court finds that sanctions are warranted for AZ's failure to produce "usable" or "reasonably accessible" documents.

Id. at *53–54. The magistrate judge elected, however, to delay a decision on the "appropriate nature and amount" of sanctions to allow the plaintiff an opportunity to present evidence and argument on any prejudice or damages caused by the failure to produce documents in a timely manner, including motion-related costs. *Id.* at *54.

Courts have also held that Rule 37(b) may be applicable where a party has discarded documents before any discovery order has been issued. *In re NTL, Inc. Securities Litigation*, 244 F.R.D. 179, 191–92 (S.D.N.Y. 2007). In this case, an adverse inference instruction and monetary payments were the sanctions chosen by the magistrate judge because the defendant either had "control" over the documents of a related corporation that did not retain the relevant e-mail or failed to preserve e-mail before the related corporation was created and assumed control over defendant's electronically stored information. *Id.* at 195–97.

Rule 37(d)

According to Rule 37(d)(3), when a party fails to produce documents demanded pursuant to Rule 34, and the requesting party moves for relief,

> Instead of or in addition to these sanctions, the court must require the party failing to act, the attorney advising that party, or both to pay the reasonable expenses, including attorney's fees, caused by the failure, unless the failure was substantially justified or other circumstances make an award of expenses unjust.

In *Bellinger v. Astrue*, 2007 WL 2907320 (E.D.N.Y. Oct. 3, 2007), searches for e-mails were not properly conducted in a timely manner. Plaintiff filed a motion to compel that was prompted in part by the incomplete and tardy e-mail production. The magistrate judge awarded plaintiff $5,000 in attorney's fees as a sanction under Rule 37(d) and later denied a motion for reconsideration.

Rule 37(e)

Rule 37(e)[8] provides:

> Absent exceptional circumstances, a court may not impose sanctions under these rules on a party for failing to provide electronically stored information lost as a result of the routine, good-faith operation of an electronic information system.

Doe v. Norwalk Community College, 2007 U.S. Dist. LEXIS 51084 (D. Conn. July 16, 2007), involved, among other problems, an uncertain

---

[8] As noted earlier, with the December 1, 2007, amendments to the Federal Rules of Civil Procedure, former Rule 37(f) is now Rule 37(e).

records retention policy for electronically stored information and a failure to suspend backup tape recycling under circumstances that warranted such suspension. A motion for sanctions was filed by the plaintiff. Defendant sought the protection of Rule 37(e). The district court rejected the argument:

> In addition, as the Commentary to Rule 37[e] indicates, the Rule only applies to information lost "due to the 'routine operation of an electronic information system'—the ways in which such systems are generally designed, programmed, and implemented to meet the party's technical and business needs." See Fed. R. Civ. P. 37[e] at Advisory Committee Notes to 2006 Amendment. This Rule therefore appears to require a routine system in order to take advantage of the good faith exception, and the court cannot find that the defendants had such a system in place. Indeed, testimony at the Hearings revealed that, after NCC shifted over to the Hartford server in August 2004, e-mails were backed up for one year; however, e-mails pre-dating this transfer were only retained for six months or less. Thus, the defendants did not appear to have one consistent, "routine" system in place, and Bissell admitted at Hearing II that the State Librarian's policy [two-year retention protocol for electronic correspondence] was not followed. Counsel for the defendants also indicated at Oral Argument that he was not aware that the defendants did anything to stop the destruction of the backup tapes after NCC's obligation to preserve arose.

Id. at *15–16.

Inherent Authority

Rule 37 may not be applicable before litigation commences or discovery is sought. *United Medical Supply Co., Inc. v. United States*, 77 Fed. Cl. 257 (2007), explains:

> [T]he majority view—and the one most easily reconciled with the terms of the rule—is that Rule 37 is narrower in scope and does not apply before the discovery regime is triggered. *See Beil v. Lakewood Eng'g & Mfg. Co.*, 15 F.3d 546, 552 (6th Cir. 1994); *Dillon v. Nissan Motor Co.*, 986 F.2d at 268–69; *Unigard Sec. Ins. Co.*, 982 F.2d at 368; *see also* Iain D. Johnson, "Federal Courts' Authority to Impose Sanctions for Prelitigation or Pre-order Spoliation of Evidence," 156 F.R.D. 313, 318 (1994) ("it is questionable whether Rule 37 provides

a federal court with authority to impose sanctions for spoliating evidence prior to a court order concerning discovery or a production request being served"). If that is true, the court must look to its inherent authority to impose, if at all, sanctions for evidence destruction that occurs between the time that the duty to preserve attaches and, at the least, the filing of a formal discovery request.

Id. at 268.

Phoenix Four, Inc. v. Strategic Resources Corp., et al., 2006 WL 1409413 (S.D.N.Y. May 23, 2006), provides an example of a failure to monitor a client's e-document production that resulted in a sanction under the court's inherent authority.

Two computer servers were moved from a defunct company office to the "SRC defendants'" new offices. An electronic search was made of the computer system in defendants' new offices and no relevant electronically stored information was located. However, the servers that had been moved from the defunct operation were not searched. *Id.* at *2. By coincidence, there was a server malfunction at the new offices and a technician was hired to solve it. The technician found a dormant drive[9] containing relevant electronically stored information. Litigation counsel, Mound Cotton, was notified and promptly produced the electronic data representing two hundred to three hundred boxes of documents. *Id.* Plaintiff filed a motion for sanctions because of the late production.

The district court confirmed the mandate to outside counsel found in *Zubulake v. UBS Warburg*, 229 F.R.D. 422 (S.D.N.Y. 2004) (*Zubulake V*): "Counsel has the duty to properly communicate with its client to ensure that 'all sources of relevant information [are] discovered.' To identify all such sources, counsel should 'become fully familiar with [its] client's document retention policies, as well as [its] client's data retention architecture.' This effort would involve communicating with information technology personnel and the key players in the litigation to understand how electronic information is stored." *Id.* at *5 (quoting 229 F.R.D. at 432).[10]

---

[9] It was "dormant" because it could not be "seen" by a computer user on the system served by the server. 2006 WL 1409413, at *2.

[10] Since *Zubulake V* reminded lawyers of their obligations to ensure the thoroughness of their clients' discovery responses, Zubulake v. UBS Warburg, 229 F.R.D. 422, 432–34 (S.D.N.Y. 2004), the case law has been unforgiving on lawyers who failed to do so. See, e.g., Cache La Poudre Feeds, LLC v. Land O'Lakes, Inc. et al., *supra*, 2007 U.S. Dist. LEXIS 15277, at *56–57 (counsel "retains an on-going responsibility to take appropriate measures to ensure that the client has provided all available information and documents which are

I quote in full the district court's discussion of the errors made by the law firm because they emphasize the seriousness of the duty of inquiry imposed on litigation counsel:

> Mound Cotton failed in its obligation to locate and timely produce the evidence stored in the server that the SRC Defendants took with them from Carnegie Hall Towers. Mound Cotton affirms that it engaged in dialogue with the defendants on the need to locate and gather paper and electronic documents. Indeed, when repeatedly questioned at oral argument on what inquiries it had made to discover electronic evidence, Mound Cotton reiterated that it had asked the defendants for all electronic and hard copy documents. But counsel's obligation is not confined to a request for documents; the duty is to search for sources of information.
>
> It appears that Mound Cotton never undertook the more methodical survey of the SRC Defendants' sources of information that Judge Scheindlin outlined in *Zubulake V*. Mound Cotton simply accepted the defendants' representation that, because SRC was no longer in operation, there were no computers or electronic collections to search. Had Mound Cotton been diligent, it might have asked—as it should have—what had happened to the computers SRC used at Carnegie Hall Towers. This question alone would have alerted Mound Cotton to the existence of the server that the defendants had taken with them from their former office. Further, Mound Cotton's obligation under *Zubulake V* extends to an inquiry as to whether information was stored on that server and, had the defendants been unable to answer that question, directing that a technician examine the server. In the case of a defunct organization such as SRC, this forensic effort would be no more than the equivalent of questioning the information technology personnel of a live enterprise about how information is stored on the organization's computer system.

Id. at *5–6.

Plaintiff sought sanctions under Fed. R. Civ. P. 37(c)(1), which, as restyled, provides: "If a party fails to provide information or identify

---

responsive to discovery requests"); *In re Seroquel, supra,* 2007 U.S. Dist. LEXIS 61287, at *44 (AstraZeneca and its counsel had a responsibility at the outset of the litigation to "take affirmative steps to monitor compliance so that all sources of discoverable information are identified and searched").

a witness as required by Rule 26(a)[11] or 26(e),[12] the party is not allowed to use that information or witness to supply evidence on a motion, at a hearing, or at a trial, unless the failure was substantially justified or is harmless." In addition to, or instead of, this preclusion sanction, a court, on motion, may impose other sanctions such as "requiring payment of reasonable expenses, including attorney's fees, caused by the failure" and "any of the sanctions authorized under Rule 37(b)(2)(A), (B), and (C)."[13] The district court decided that Rule 37(c)(1) sanctions were inappropriate in part because the documents in question were ultimately found and produced. *Id.* at *8–9.

However, the district court awarded monetary sanctions under its inherent authority. Both the SRC defendants and Mound Cotton were ordered to reimburse Phoenix equally for costs and fees associated with the filing of the motion for sanctions. The district court had to approve the amount once time records were produced. They were ordered to pay $10,000 each for the redepositions of three witnesses for the limited purpose of inquiring into issues raised by the documents recovered from the

---

[11] Rule 26(a) governs disclosures, including initial disclosures, disclosure of expert testimony, and pretrial disclosures. Among the required initial disclosures are "a copy—or a description by category and location—of all documents, electronically stored information, and tangible things that the disclosing party has in its possession, custody, or control and may use to support its claims or defenses, unless the use would be solely for impeachment." Fed. R. Civ. P. 26(a)(1)(A)(ii).

[12] Rule 26(e)(1) provides: "A party who has made a disclosure under Rule 26(a)—or who has responded to an interrogatory, request for production, or request for admission—must supplement or correct its disclosure or response: (A) in a timely manner if the party learns that in some material respect the disclosure or response is incomplete or incorrect, and if the additional or corrective information has not otherwise been made known to the other parties during the discovery process or in writing; or (B) as ordered by the court." Rule 26(e)(2) relates to expert witnesses and provides: "For an expert whose report must be disclosed under Rule 26(a)(2)(B), the party's duty to supplement extends both to information included in the report and to information given during the expert's deposition. Any additions or changes to this information must be disclosed by the time the party's pretrial disclosures under Rule 26(a)(3) are due."

[13] Rule 37(b)(2) authorizes a court to issue sanctions for disobeying discovery orders. Rule 37(b)(2)(A) and (C) are quoted in full at n. 7. Rule 37(b)(2)(B) provides: "If a party fails to comply with an order under Rule 35(a) requiring it to produce another person for examination, the court may issue any of the orders listed in Rule 37(b)(2)(A)(i)–(vi), unless the disobedient party shows that it cannot produce the other person." See, e.g., Arista Records, LLC v. Tschirhart, 241 F.R.D. 462 (W.D. Tex. 2006) (default judgment entered as sanction under Rule 37(b)(2) and inherent authority of the court after defendant used "wiping software" to remove material data from her hard drive before a court-ordered forensic inspection of the hard drive was about to occur).

server. The district court also ordered that the SRC defendants' shares could not be paid by their insurers. *Id.* at *9.

Lawyers may not be seeking indemnities from their clients after *Phoenix Four,* but the importance of e-discovery due diligence cannot be overemphasized in light of this decision.[14]

---

[14] Litigants should be alert to discovery deadlines in federal court in relation to obligations to produce electronically stored information. The more complex the case, and the shorter the discovery period allowed by court order, the more likely it is that e-discovery will have to be conducted rapidly. Where there are a number of witnesses to be deposed, documents will be sought to accommodate lawyers' needs to review them in time to adequately prepare for depositions. Generally speaking, in the world of electronically stored information "haste makes waste," and "waste" can mean sanctions. In symmetric cases, where both sides have equal e-discovery burdens, reasonable solutions will be agreed upon. In "asymmetric" cases, where one side has electronically stored information and the other does not, reasonable solutions may not be reached for tactical reasons. Courts who follow Rule 1's mandate will address unreasonable positions taken by requesting parties. But in cases where large amounts of electronically stored information are involved, producing parties need to account for the time to identify, locate, and collect potentially responsive electronic documents; review the documents for relevance, privilege in whole or in part (and to redact if privileged in part), and confidentiality designations; make appropriate objections; and produce responsive documents. In a matter with tight discovery deadlines, these tasks might have to occur within two to three months. Identifying and contracting with reputable, dependable vendors is not a facile process for the inexperienced, and good vendors may not be available when needed. These cases demonstrate that there is no substitute for proper planning, preparation, and execution in the area of sanctions avoidance.

CHAPTER EIGHT

Does *Qualcomm* Answer the Question of Whether You Can Take Comfort in the Fact That *Morgan Stanley* Was Vacated?

Morgan Stanley & Co. v. Coleman (Parent) Holdings, Inc., 955 So. 2d 1124 (Fla. 4th Dist. Ct. App. 2007), *petition for rev. denied* 973 So. 2d 1120 (Fla. 2007),[1] was every litigant's worst nightmare. Morgan Stanley failed

---

[1] The order denying review can be found at: www.floridasupremecourt.org/pub_info/summaries/briefs/07/07-1251/Filed_12-12-2007_Order_Dismissing.pdf.

to locate and search all of its backup tapes in a timely fashion and had untruthfully certified compliance with an order that it had found them all. Based on the circuit court's findings, Morgan Stanley had engaged in deliberate efforts to mislead the plaintiff and the court about compliance with its electronic and nonelectronic discovery obligations. The circuit court ultimately entered a default judgment against Morgan Stanley, and the jury awarded plaintiff $604,334,000 in compensatory damages and $850,000,000 in punitive damages. Yes, the judgment was vacated in a 2–1 decision—but on other grounds. The majority opinion did not comment on the sanctions. The dissenting opinion said that implicit in the majority decision was that the sanctions were appropriate.[2]

Just when the *Morgan Stanley* case was finally exiting the e-discovery seminar circuit, along came the *Qualcomm* case.

Qualcomm Inc. v. Broadcom Corp., 2008 WL 66932 (S.D. Cal. Jan. 7, 2008), involved a patent infringement claim brought by Qualcomm based on Broadcom's manufacture and sale of "H.264-compliant" products. H.264 is a standard for video compression that was set by a standards-setting body called the Joint Video Team (JVT). Broadcom defended the action in part by claiming Qualcomm's H.264-related patents were unenforceable due to inequitable conduct or waiver. The waiver claim was predicated on Qualcomm's participation in JVT. Hence, Broadcom sought in discovery information about Qualcomm's participation in the JVT. Qualcomm served discovery responses saying it would provide such information to the extent it could be located and was not privileged. *Id.* at 1–2.

Qualcomm was later served with a Rule 30(b)(6) deposition notice. It produced a witness, Christine Irvine, whose computer was never searched for relevant documents and who was not provided with JVT-related documents. She testified that Qualcomm was not involved with the JVT. She was then promptly impeached with documents showing Qualcomm was involved with the JVT. Qualcomm later decided to provide a new Rule 30(b)(6) witness. This second corporate designee also apparently was not prepared well and his computer was not searched. He testified that Qualcomm became involved with the JVT in late 2003 *after* the H.264 standard had been published. Broadcom attempted to impeach the witness with a 2002 e-mail list from the Advanced Video Coding (AVC) ad hoc group within the JVT that contained a Qualcomm e-mail address (viji@qualcomm.com). *Id.* at *3. This address belonged to

---

[2] "I agree that the trial court did not abuse its discretion in the sanctions imposed on Morgan Stanley for substantial violations of court orders." 955 So. 2d at 1133, n.4. (Farmer, J. dissenting).

Viji Raveendran, a Qualcomm employee. The presence of a Qualcomm employee's e-mail on the list suggested that Qualcomm "was receiving JVT/AVC reports in 2002." *Id.* at *3, n.2. The witness, however, did not recognize the document. *Id.* at *3.

Broadcom continued to insist then and thereafter that the list was evidence of Qualcomm's involvement in the H.264 standard-setting process. However, Qualcomm "became increasingly aggressive" in arguing the opposite: that it had not participated in the JVT while the H.264 standard was being developed. *Id.* This argument was critical to both sides because proof of participation by Qualcomm in the JVT in 2002 "would have prohibited Qualcomm from suing companies, including Broadcom, that utilized the H.264 standard" because such participation would have required Qualcomm to license patents that "reasonably may be essential to the practice of the H.264 standard" either royalty-free or under nondiscriminatory reasonable terms. *Id.*

The trial commenced on January 9, 2007. From its opening statement forward, Qualcomm maintained the position that it had not participated in the JVT in 2002 and early 2003 when the H.264 standard was being created. Ms. Raveendran was a witness and was being prepared to testify by Adam Bier. Mr. Bier submitted a declaration explaining that in the course of the preparation, he discovered an August 2, 2002, e-mail to her welcoming her to the AVC mailing list. On January 14, 2007, he searched her laptop and found twenty one separate e-mails relating to the AVC, none of which had been produced in discovery. The e-mail chains "bore several dates in November 2002 and the authors discussed various issues relating to the H.264 standard." *Id.* at *4. Ms. Raveendran was not a named author or recipient on the e-mails. She received them by virtue of her status of being on the list.

"The Qualcomm trial team decided not to produce these newly discovered e-mails to Broadcom, claiming that they were not responsive to Broadcom's discovery requests." *Id.* Those chilling words were followed by two other outcome-determinative observations of the magistrate:

> The attorneys ignored the fact that the presence of the e-mails on Raveendran's computer undercut Qualcomm's premier argument that it had not participated in the JVT in 2002. The Qualcomm trial team failed to conduct any investigation to determine whether there were more e-mails that also had not been produced.

Id. (record citation omitted).

Making matters worse, Qualcomm's trial counsel, on January 18, 2007, argued at a sidebar conference against the admission of the AVC list telling the district court that "there are no e-mails...there's no evidence that any e-mail was actually sent to this list." *Id.* "None of the Qualcomm attorneys who were present during the sidebar mentioned" the twenty-one AVC-related e-mails found on Ms. Raveendran's computer on January 14, 2007, the magistrate observed. *Id.*

Ms. Raveendran was called as a witness by Qualcomm. On cross-examination, she admitted that she had received e-mails because she was on the list. After initially questioning before the district court whether they were responsive, Qualcomm later the same day produced the twenty-one e-mails. *Id.* at *4–5.

On January 26, 2007, the jury returned verdicts, including one that the Qualcomm patents were not enforceable due to waiver. *Id.* at *5. Following the trial, Broadcom pursued what it believed to be discovery violations. On February 16, 2007, Qualcomm's counsel, Mr. Bier, wrote to Broadcom's counsel saying that "we continue to believe" that Qualcomm performed a reasonable search and insisting that the twenty-one e-mails were not responsive to a discovery request. After a demand for a further search was made by Broadcom, on March 7, 2007, Mr. Bier wrote saying that Broadcom's characterization of Qualcomm's discovery performance was "wholly without merit," but that Qualcomm would conduct a search of current and archived e-mails for five trial witnesses using the search terms "JVT," "avc-ce," and "H.264." *Id.* at *6.

On April 9, 2007, Qualcomm's lead trial counsel and general counsel jointly wrote to the district court admitting that Qualcomm had thousands of relevant unproduced documents. Qualcomm's review of the documents "revealed facts that appear to be inconsistent with certain arguments that [counsel] made on Qualcomm's behalf at trial and in the equitable hearing following trial." *Id.* An apology was included in the letter.

As of June 28, 2007, Qualcomm had searched the e-mail archives of twenty-one employees and located 46,000 documents representing more than 300,000 pages that were responsive to Broadcom's discovery requests but not produced. *Id.* Qualcomm later found three additional e-mails that were produced on August 7, 2007. *Id.*

In an August 6, 2007, order, the district court determined that Qualcomm had wrongfully concealed its patents while participating in the JVT and then hid this concealment "from the Court, the jury, and opposing counsel during the present litigation." *Id.* at *5 (quoting the district court's order). The district court further found that Qualcomm's counsel participated in "an organized program of litigation misconduct and concealment throughout discovery, trial, and post-trial before new counsel took over lead role in the case on April 27, 2007." *Id.* (same).

The district court granted Broadcom's motion for attorneys' fees under 28 U.S.C. §285,[3] but separately determined that Qualcomm's discovery misconduct justified payment of Broadcom's attorneys' fees, court costs, expert witness fees, travel expenses, and any other litigation costs reasonably incurred by Broadcom. *Id.* The district court later accepted the magistrate's recommendation under Section 285 to require Qualcomm to pay Broadcom $8,568,633.24 in defense costs plus postjudgment interest at 4.91 percent from August 6, 2007, resulting in a total award of $9,259,985.09. *Id.*

Broadcom's sanction motion sought reimbursement of defense costs to the extent not awarded under Section 285; a fine payable to the court; a requirement that Qualcomm implement a discovery program to prevent future litigation misconduct; and identification of "all false statements and arguments." *Id.* at *17.

In discussing the authority to award sanctions, the magistrate cited to Rules 37(a), 37(b), 37(c)(1), and 26(g), as well as its inherent authority. However, the magistrate explained that Rules 37(a) and (b) did not apply because Broadcom did not file a motion to compel. It did not do so because Qualcomm said it would produce responsive documents and then did not, unbeknownst to Broadcom. *Id.* at 8.[4] That prompted the magistrate to pronounce:

> For the current "good faith" discovery system to function in the electronic age, attorneys and clients must work together to ensure that both understand how and where electronic documents, records and e-mails are maintained and to determine how best to locate, review, and produce responsive documents. Attorneys must take responsibility for ensuring that their clients conduct a comprehensive and appropriate document search. Producing 1.2 million pages of marginally relevant documents while hiding 46,000 critically important ones does not constitute good faith and does not satisfy either the client's or attorney's discovery obligations. Similarly, agreeing to produce certain categories of documents and then not producing all of the documents that fit within such a category is unacceptable. Qualcomm's conduct warrants sanctions.

---

[3] Section 285 applies to patent cases and reads in full: "The court in exceptional cases may award reasonable attorney fees to the prevailing party."

[4] Qualcomm sought to "capitalize" on this failure in its response to the motion for sanctions, prompting this response from the magistrate: "This argument is indicative of the gamesmanship Qualcomm engaged in throughout this litigation." 2008 WL 66932 at *8, n.4.

Id. at *9. The magistrate then proceeded to find:

- Qualcomm "intentionally withheld documents" based on its failure to produce the documents, search for the documents, produce the twenty-one e-mails from Ms. Raveendran's computer, search for additional e-mails after the twenty-one e-mails were found, and conduct after trial an internal investigation to determine if there were additional unproduced documents; and based on its resisting Broadcom's efforts to force such a search. *Id.* at *10.
- Qualcomm's claim of "inadvertence" was "negated by the massive volume and direct relevance of the hidden documents." *Id.* And even if Qualcomm did not know about the "suppressed e-mails," there were warning signs that should have alerted Qualcomm to the inadequacy of the production, the magistrate said. Illustratively, many of the suppressed e-mails were sent to or from Ms. Irvine, the first 30(b)(6) witness who testified that Qualcomm was never involved with the JVT, and Qualcomm had not searched her computer before she was deposed. *Id.* at *10–11.
- Qualcomm did not intentionally hide from its lawyers the documents or did not hide them so effectively that that "the lawyers did not know or suspect that the suppressed documents existed." *Id.* at *12.
- Qualcomm's lawyers were not inept or disorganized, and therefore neither was an excuse for their failure to discover "the intentionally hidden documents or suspect their existence." *Id.*
- There was no evidence demonstrating that Qualcomm shared the "damaging documents" with its retained attorneys and they worked together to hide the documents, and the magistrate refused to infer knowledge given the invocation of the attorney-client privilege by Qualcomm.[5] *Id.* at *12–13.
- Instead, one or more of the retained attorneys chose

---

[5] In a footnote, the magistrate explained that Qualcomm invoked the attorney-client privilege as to its communications with its retained counsel so that they were not part of the record. Retained counsel complained that they were unable to provide information about their conduct as a result of the privilege bar, to no avail. Their concern was "heightened" when Qualcomm submitted "self-serving declarations describing the failings of its retained lawyers." The magistrate drew no adverse inferences from the invocation of the privilege but said that the "fact remains that the Court does not have access to all of the information necessary to reach an informed decision regarding the actual knowledge of the attorneys." 2008 WL 66932 at *13, n.8.

not to look in the correct locations for the correct documents, to accept the unsubstantiated assurances of an important client that its search was sufficient, to ignore the warning signs that the document search and production were inadequate, not to press Qualcomm employees for the truth, and/or to encourage employees to provide the information (or lack of information) that Qualcomm needed to assert its nonparticipation argument and to succeed in this lawsuit.

Id. at *13.

The magistrate then identified six lawyers who failed to meet their obligations and were sanctioned under Rule 26(g) or the inherent power of the court. Three of them, including lead counsel, handled or supervised Qualcomm's discovery responses and production of documents. They failed to make a reasonable inquiry into "Qualcomm's discovery search and production and their conduct contributed to the discovery violation." *Id.* at *13. Two others, plus one of the original three, "did not perform a reasonable inquiry to determine whether Qualcomm had complied with its discovery obligations." *Id.* at *14. One other, plus lead counsel and the lawyer that supervised Bier (who found the twenty-one e-mails on Ms. Raveendran's computer), "bear responsibility for the discovery failure because they did not conduct a reasonable inquiry into Qualcomm's discovery production before making specific factual and legal arguments to the court." *Id.* As to one lawyer, the magistrate wrote:

Patch was an integral part of the trial team—familiar with Qualcomm's arguments, theories and strategies. He knew on January 14th that 21 avc_ce e-mails had been discovered on Raveendran's computer. Without reading or reviewing the e-mails, Patch participated in the decision not to produce them. Several days later, Patch carefully tailored his questions to ensure that Raveendran did not testify about the unproduced e-mails. And, after Broadcom stumbled into the e-mail testimony, Patch affirmatively misled the Court by claiming that he did not know whether the e-mails were responsive to Broadcom's discovery requests. This conduct is unacceptable and, considering the totality of the circumstances, it is unrealistic to think that Patch did not know or believe that Qualcomm's document search was inadequate and that Qualcomm possessed numerous, similar and unproduced documents.

Id. at *15.

Thirteen additional lawyers, including local counsel who on behalf of others and for logistical reasons signed papers containing false statements,[6] were spared sanctions by the magistrate. *Id.* at *15–16.

As sanctions, the magistrate awarded Broadcom all of its litigation fees and costs subject to a setoff for the amounts paid by Qualcomm, under the Section 285 fee award. *Id.* at *17. The magistrate declined to fine Qualcomm, given the amount of the attorneys' fee award. *Id.* at *17,[7] n.17.[8] The six sanctioned lawyers were referred to the State Bar of California "for appropriate investigation and possible imposition of sanctions." *Id.* at *18.

Five Qualcomm lawyers[9] and the sanctioned lawyers were also ordered to participate in a Comprehensive Case Review and Enforcement of Discovery Obligations (CREDO) program. The magistrate emphasized that in requiring this program, the magistrate was not seeking the identities of individuals who contributed to discovery failures or the content of privileged communications. However, the CREDO protocol "must include a *detailed analysis*," *Id.* at 19 (emphasis in original):

> (1) identifying the factors that contributed to the discovery violation (e.g., insufficient communication (including between client and retained counsel, among retained lawyers and law firms, and between junior lawyers conducting discovery and senior lawyers asserting legal arguments); inadequate case management (within Qualcomm, between Qualcomm and the retained lawyers, and by the retained lawyers); inadequate discovery plans (within Qualcomm and between Qualcomm and its retained attorneys); etc.),

---

[6] In a footnote, the magistrate wrote: "[T]he Court notes that sanctioning local counsel for such conduct is possible and may be imposed in another case under different circumstances. Attorneys must remember that they are required to conduct a reasonable inquiry into the accuracy of the pleadings prior to signing, filing or arguing them." 2008 WL 66932 at *16, n.14.

[7] The sanction has since been paid by Qualcomm. Reply to Broadcom Corporation's Response to Objections of Responding Attorneys to Sanctions Order of Magistrate Judge, p. 1 (Case 3:05-cv-01958-B-BLM; Document 741, filed Feb. 20, 2008).

[8] The magistrate also elected not to impose monetary sanctions against the sanctioned lawyers. Among the reasons were these two: "First, if the imposed sanctions do not convince the attorneys to behave in a more ethical and professional manner in the future, monetary sanctions are unlikely to do so. Second, it is possible that Qualcomm will seek contribution from its retained attorneys after it pays Broadcom's attorneys' fees and costs and, in light of that significant monetary sanction, an additional fine is unlikely to affect counsel's future behavior." 2008 WL 66932 at *18, n.18.

[9] "Qualcomm chose not to provide any information to the Court regarding the actions of Qualcomm's counsel or employees so the Court must rely on the retained attorneys' statements that these attorneys were involved in the case." 2008 WL 66932 at *18, n.19.

(2) creating and evaluating proposals, procedures, and processes that will correct the deficiencies identified in subsection (1),

(3) developing and finalizing a comprehensive protocol that will prevent future discovery violations (e.g., determining the depth and breadth of case management and discovery plans that should be adopted; identifying by experience or authority the attorney from the retained counsel's office who should interface with the corporate counsel and on which issues; describing the frequency the attorneys should meet and whether other individuals should participate in the communications; identifying who should participate in the development of the case management and discovery plans; describing and evaluating various methods of resolving conflicts and disputes between the client and retained counsel, especially relating to the adequacy of discovery searches; describing the type, nature, frequency, and participants in case management and discovery meetings; and, suggesting required ethical and discovery training; etc.),

(4) applying the protocol that was developed in subsection (3) to other factual situations, such as when the client does not have corporate counsel, when the client has a single in-house lawyer, when the client has a large legal staff, and when there are two law firms representing one client,

(5) identifying and evaluating data tracking systems, software, or procedures that corporations could implement to better enable inside and outside counsel to identify potential sources of discoverable documents (e.g. the correct databases, archives, etc.), and

(6) any other information or suggestions that will help prevent discovery violations.

Id. at *19. The magistrate said that a Broadcom lawyer "may participate in the process. If Broadcom decides to participate, Qualcomm and the Sanctioned Attorneys must pay the Broadcom attorney's reasonable costs and fees incurred in traveling to and participating in this program." *Id.* at *19, n.21.

The sanctioned and Qualcomm lawyers were required to meet with the magistrate to facilitate development of the CREDO program. The magistrate added: "The Court will provide whatever time is necessary for the participants to fully and completely examine, analyze and complete the CREDO protocol." *Id.* at *19. The magistrate further explained that once the protocol was found sufficient by the magistrate, it would be filed and each of the lawyers in the CREDO program then "shall each file a declaration under penalty of perjury affirming that they personally participated in the entire process that led to the CREDO protocol and specifying the amount of time they spent working on it." *Id.*

The magistrate's closing remarks were reminiscent of the trial court's comment in the *Morgan Stanley* case ("the judicial system cannot function this way"):[10]

> While no one can undo the misconduct in this case, this process, hopefully, will establish a baseline for other cases. Perhaps it also will establish a turning point in what the Court perceives as a decline in and deterioration of civility, professionalism and ethical conduct in the litigation arena. To the extent it does so, everyone benefits—Broadcom, Qualcomm, and all attorneys who engage in, and judges who preside over, complex litigation. If nothing else, it will provide a road map to assist counsel and corporate clients in complying with their ethical and discovery obligations and conducting the requisite "reasonable inquiry."

Id. at *20.

As noted above, the six sanctioned lawyers were not permitted by the magistrate judge to use attorney-client privileged communications to defend themselves. They appealed the magistrate's decision in this regard. The district court agreed with the six sanctioned attorneys and vacated this portion of the magistrate's order to permit the attorneys to put on evidence, presumably about who was responsible for the failure to produce the electronically stored information during discovery. 2008 WL 638108, *3 (S.D. Calif. March 5, 2008). In words that should give no comfort to either the six sanctioned attorneys or the Qualcomm attorneys, whose actions, presumably, will be the focus of the sanctioned attorneys' defense, the district court told the magistrate judge that her discretion "regarding responsibility and sanctions, if any, are not limited, either upwardly or downwardly, by the Order of Remand." *Id.* at *2.

There is no substitute for e-discovery due diligence. Clients must get their e-discovery house in order. Outside counsel must make sure that the house is in order. And outside counsel should not make representations to a court without being assured of the facts nor make statements without any qualification if they are not assured of the facts nor agree to language in a court order that the client cannot satisfy. As *Qualcomm* sadly demonstrates, from an e-discovery perspective, no one should take comfort in the ultimate outcome of *Morgan Stanley*.

---

[10] Coleman (Parent) Holdings, Inc., v. Morgan Stanley & Co., Inc., Case No. 502003, p. 16 (Fla. 15th Jud. Cir., Mar. 23, 2005), which can be found at www.lexisnexis.com/applied discovery/lawlibrary/Order.pdf.

CHAPTER NINE

Must Bad Faith Be Shown to Obtain Sanctions against the United States?

The answer is no.

In *United Medical Supply Co., Inc. v. United States*, 77 Fed. Cl. 257 (2007), United Medical Supply (UMS) alleged that the United States breached a contract by failing to buy from plaintiff medical supplies and equipment that were destined for use at U.S. military medical treatment facilities (MTFs). UMS sought discovery of documents, and, in particular, credit card receipts, relating to purchases by the MTFs from other sources of medical supplies. The Defense Supply Center (DSC) lawyer assigned to the matter initiated a litigation hold via e-mail, but, because of incorrect e-mail addresses, failed to reach some MTFs. The litigation hold notice provided that recipients should confirm their receipt of the hold notice, but the DSC lawyer did not verify with any MTF whether the e-mail had been received and did not contact MTFs that did not respond. *Id.* at 259–60. Relevant documents were destroyed because the hold notice either did not reach an MTF or because recipients did not understand what they were supposed to retain. *Id.* at 261–62. A sanctions motion followed.

The United States admitted it had a duty to preserve relevant documents and that it violated that duty. It urged the court, however, to reject the sanctions motions because it did not act in bad faith. *Id.* at 264.

The court concluded that bad faith need not be shown to impose spoliation sanctions. *Id.* at 268. The court explained:

> Requiring a showing of bad faith as a precondition to the imposition of spoliation sanctions means that evidence may be destroyed willfully, or through gross negligence or even reckless disregard, without any true consequences. At least in Hohfeldian terms, in which a duty is the jural correlate of a right, this approach is tantamount to suggesting that the "duty" to preserve evidence is not much of a duty at all. Second, imposing sanctions only when a spoliator can be proven to have acted in bad faith defenestrates three of the four purposes underlying such sanctions—to protect the integrity of the fact-finding process, to restore the adversarial balance between the spoliator and the prejudiced party, and to deter future misconduct—and severely frustrates the last, to punish. These objectives are hardly served if the court, in effect, is constrained to say to the injured party—"sorry about that, but there is nothing I can do, except to let you present your case, such as it remains."

Id. at 268–69 (footnotes and citations omitted).

The court found that the United States had not only spoliated relevant documents but, as often seems to occur in spoliation cases, also misled the court about its compliance with the court's November 18, 2005, discovery order, *id.* at 271–72, and concluded that the government had acted in reckless disregard of its duty to preserve. *Id.* at 274. The court imposed two sanctions. First, the United States was prohibited from cross-examining plaintiff's expert to the extent that the expert extrapolated information favorably to plaintiff to fill gaps in records resulting from the spoliation. Second, the United States was obliged to "reimburse plaintiff for any additional discovery-related costs, including attorney's fees, that were incurred after November 18, 2005, because of defendant's malfeasance and misrepresentations, as well as all the costs, including attorney's fees, that were incurred in specifically pursuing this spoliation matter." *Id.* at 276.

CHAPTER TEN

Must Bad Faith Be Shown to Obtain Sanctions against a Party Other Than the United States?

The answer is: it depends on your forum, the type of sanction sought, and the degree of prejudice.

United Medical Supply contains an excellent survey of the case law in the federal circuit and circuit courts of appeal regarding the division of authority on what level of conduct is required before a spoliation-related sanction can be imposed on a producing party.

> On one end of that spectrum, actually representing a distinct minority, are courts that require a showing of bad faith before any form of sanction is applied. Other courts expect such a showing, but only for the imposition of certain more serious sanctions, such as the application of an adverse inference or the entry of a default judgment. Further relaxing the scienter requirement, some courts do not require a showing of bad faith, but do require proof of purposeful, willful or intentional conduct, at least as to certain sanctions, so as not to impose sanctions based solely upon negligent conduct. On

the other side of the spectrum, we find courts that do not require a showing of purposeful conduct, at all, but instead require merely that there be a showing of fault, with the degree of fault, ranging from mere negligence to bad faith, impacting the severity of the sanction. If this continuum were not complicated enough, some circuits initially appear to have adopted universal rules, only to later shade their precedents with caveats. Other times, the difference between decisions appear to be more a matter of semantics, perhaps driven by state law, with some courts, for example, identifying as "bad faith" what others would call "recklessness" or even "gross negligence."

Id. at **28–29 (footnotes omitted). *See also* Barkett, "The Prelitigation Duty to Preserve: Look Out!" (ABA Annual Meeting, Chicago, August 2005)[1] (discussing, circuit by circuit, the varying jurisprudence on the level of conduct required to obtain an adverse inference instruction).

One day, the Supreme Court or the Civil Rules Advisory Committee will straighten out the conflicting case law. In the meantime, if you are seeking sanctions against a party, know your jurisdiction's jurisprudence.

---

[1] An updated version of this article is available at www.shb.com/shb.asp?pgid=929& attorney_id=276&st=f, under "Speeches."

CHAPTER ELEVEN

Identification of Key Players: How Far Do You Cast the Net?

A challenge facing all litigants is the timely identification of "key players"—that is, custodians of relevant electronically stored information[1]—in relation to the preservation of such information. *Consol. Aluminum Corp. v. Alcoa, Inc.*, 2006 U.S. Dist. LEXIS 66642 (M.D. La. July 19, 2006), illustrates the risk. Alcoa sent a cost-recovery demand to Consolidated Aluminum in 2002 and promptly put a litigation hold on the electronic documents of four Alcoa employees involved with a remedial investigation and cleanup. In 2003, Consolidated filed a declaratory judgment action seeking to be absolved of liability.

In 2005, Consolidated propounded discovery that prompted Alcoa to expand its key player list by eleven more names. It was not until this expansion that Alcoa suspended its janitorial e-mail deletion policy and backup tape maintenance policy, which at Alcoa meant that e-mail

---

[1] The importance of preserving information in relation to "key players" is highlighted by Zubulake v. UBS Warburg LLC, 2004 U.S. Dist. LEXIS 13574 (S.D.N.Y. July 20, 2004) (*Zubulake V*), in which the district court made seventeen references to "key," "players," or "employees" in an e-discovery sanctions setting where the district court decided to issue an adverse inference instruction because of the failure to preserve electronic information.

older than about seven months was no longer available unless it had been archived by the individual user. The magistrate judge sanctioned Alcoa—in effect determining that Alcoa should have identified these additional individuals as key players in 2002.[2] The magistrate's decision had a context. One of the "newly identified" key players, Blair, had been the subject of a motion for Alcoa to take his deposition early in the litigation because he was aged and a critical witness. Yet Alcoa downplayed Mr. Blair's importance in response to the motion for sanctions. The magistrate found these positions incongruous, which hurt Alcoa's credibility before the magistrate on the "key player" issue.[3]

The facts were somewhat similar in *E*Trade Sec. LLC v. Deutsche Bank AG*, 230 F.R.D. 582 (D. Minn. 2005), where the district court adopted the opinion of the magistrate judge. A defendant, NSI, failed to place a litigation hold on the auto-deletion of e-mail because, it said, any deleted e-mail would be retained on backup tapes. However, the backup tapes were retained only for three years. In 2001, when litigation between the parties first arose, key employees were identified. In 2004, NSI identified additional employees whose e-mail needed to be searched. However, the backup tapes containing the e-mail of these employees would have been

---

[2] The district court declined to impose an adverse inference instruction sanction on Alcoa, but ordered Alcoa to bear the cost of redeposing the eleven new key players, among others, as well as "any other employees of Alcoa later determined to be 'key players' in this litigation whose e-mails have not been preserved" and to pay the costs and fees associated with the motion for sanctions and "in investigating and attempting to obtain the discovery in issue." 2006 U.S. Dist. LEXIS 66642, at *36.

[3] The magistrate described Alcoa's assertion that the only pertinent information Mr. Blair had with respect to the case related to his historical knowledge of the facility, "which can only be obtained through deposition testimony as to his memory of events, not through contemporary documents or e-mails." 2006 U.S. Dist. LEXIS 66642, at *14. The magistrate juxtaposed this position against Alcoa's statements when Alcoa moved to take Blair's deposition early. Alcoa wrote then that Mr. Blair's memory of events is "critical to Alcoa's defense and to its counterclaim," that if it were unable to take Mr. Blair's deposition early, that "could lead to 'severe prejudice' to Alcoa if some 'untoward event' were to befall Mr. Blair"; and that Mr. Blair possesses "critical information about the raw materials, usage, manufacturing processes, and waste handling/disposal practices of Consolidated." *Id.* at *14–15. The magistrate then concluded: "In the Court's view, these statements by Alcoa indicate that Mr. Blair is one of the 'key players' in this litigation who was likely to have relevant information in his e-mails which Alcoa had a duty to preserve from the time this litigation became reasonably anticipated, even if he was a plant level employee who was not directly involved in the ongoing environmental investigation. In other words, the Court finds that Alcoa conceded, early on, that Mr. Blair is a 'key player' in this litigation and is now attempting to rescind that statement because of its failure to instruct him to preserve evidence." *Id.* at *15.

overwritten because backup tapes were retained only for three years. As a result, relevant e-mail messages from 2001 and earlier were "irretrievably destroyed." *Id.* at 592. After finding that the plaintiff was prejudiced by the loss of e-mail, the district court concluded that NSI committed spoliation by not placing an adequate litigation hold on e-mail boxes and by failing to make changes in its backup tape three-year retention policy. *Id.* This decision also has a credibility context. A related defendant was faulted for wiping clean hard drives on all computers after the duty to preserve arose.[4] *Id.* at 589. This same defendant failed to preserve audio recordings of its securities traders, which would have been relevant to the claim of a possible fraudulent trading scheme of the securities that were at issue. *Id.* at 590. Because of these preservation violations, and because prejudice was found to exist,[5] the district court accepted the magistrate's recommendation that an adverse inference instruction should be issued as a sanction. *Id.* at 585, 593.

A litigant should always cast the key-player net wisely. A wisely cast net need not be a widely cast net. Litigants should use the Rule 26(f) meet-and-confer session and the Rule 16 conference to achieve an agreement on the breadth of "key players." Litigants should understand that their credibility before a court can impact a court's decision making:

---

[4] This defendant explained that it was shutting down the business and was going to give the computers to the employees and wipe the computers clean to eliminate any confidential information on the hard drives. 230 F.R.D. at 589.

[5] "All the information contained on the hard drives has been irretrievably destroyed. In addition, recorded telephone conversations have been destroyed by failing to retain the calls at an appropriate time. Evidence in the record demonstrates that Reed was actively involved in the borrowing/lending of GENI, ICII and RVEE securities. Plaintiffs' cases rely on evidence indicating Nomura Canada's knowledge of the activities of its employee Reed with respect to the securities transactions. Internal documents saved on individuals' hard drives, especially Reed's supervisor, would have provided evidence of the extent of Nomura Canada's knowledge and acceptance of Reed's actions. Here, there is a reasonable probability that the loss of the evidence stored on the hard drives of the Nomura Canada employees and the evidence in the recorded telephone conversations has materially prejudiced the plaintiffs in their case against the Nomura Defendants." *Id.* at 592. "The court also finds that relevant e-mail was deleted by NSI's failure to place a litigation hold on mailboxes or preserve the backup tapes for the relevant time period. E-mail messages in the record demonstrate that there are internal communications that shed light on the compan[y's] knowledge of Reed's actions in the Stock Lending Group and measure the company took after notice of the problems with the transactions. NSI itself has identified additional mail boxes it deemed relevant to search for this litigation but failed to preserve at an earlier date. This destruction of potentially relevant evidence has prejudiced the plaintiffs in presenting their case about NSI's involvement in and knowledge of the transactions in question." *Id.* (record citation omitted).

demanding too many key players is as indefensible as offering too few key players. Courts should not fault litigants for making reasonable decisions on the number of appropriate custodians of electronically stored information based on the information reasonably available at the time the decisions are made.

CHAPTER TWELVE

Are Document Retention Notices and Keyword Search Protocols Discoverable?

The answers can be complicated. Document retention notices are protected from production. However, what may not be discoverable in the abstract still may be voluntarily produced by a party, arguably at the risk of a subject-matter privilege waiver. And while unilateral keyword searches are work product, there are document productions where they should be collaborative.

Let's start with document retention notices (DRNs). In *Gibson v. Ford Motor Co.*, 2007 WL 41954, at *6 (N.D. Ga. Jan. 4, 2007), the district court rejected a plaintiff's demand for copies of Ford's litigation hold notices:

> In the Court's experience, these instructions are often, if not always, drafted by counsel, involve their work product, are often overly inclusive, and the documents they list do not necessarily bear a reasonable relationship to the issues in litigation. This is not a document relating to the Defendant's business. Rather, the document relates exclusively to this litigation, was apparently created after

this dispute arose, and exists for the sole purpose of assuring compliance with discovery that may be required in this litigation. Not only is the document likely to constitute attorney work-product, but its compelled production could dissuade other businesses from issuing such instructions in the event of litigation. Instructions like the one that appears to have been issued here insure the availability of information during litigation. Parties should be encouraged, not discouraged, to issue such directives. Defendants are not required to produce these materials.

Similarly, the magistrate judge in *In re eBay Seller Antitrust Litigation*, 2007 WL 2852364 (N.D. Cal. Oct. 2, 2007), refused to order production of the DRNs because they were shown to be protected under the attorney-client and work-product privileges. However, the magistrate ordered eBay to disclose the names of six hundred employees who received the litigation hold notice. *Id.* at *3. The magistrate considered the relevance of the identities of the six hundred employees to be tenuous, but found that eBay had not shown that producing the information would be burdensome or otherwise objectionable. *Id.* at *3. The magistrate also permitted discovery on the facts regarding eBay's retention and collection policies:

> eBay has made an adequate showing that the DRN documents themselves include material protected under attorney client privilege and the work product doctrine. To the extent, however, that eBay is seeking to foreclose any inquiry into the contents of those notices at deposition or through other means, such a position is not tenable. Although plaintiffs may not be entitled to probe into what exactly eBay's employees were told by its attorneys,[1] they are certainly entitled to know what eBay's employees are doing with respect to collecting and preserving ESI. Furthermore, because it would neither be reasonable nor practical to require or even to permit plaintiffs to depose all 600 employees, it is appropriate to permit plaintiffs to discover what those employees are supposed to be doing. Even though such inquiry may, indirectly, implicate communications from counsel to the employees, the focus can and should be on the facts of what eBay's document retention and collection policies are, rather than on any details of the DRNs. Thus, while plaintiffs should not inquire specifically into how the DRNs

---

[1] In a footnote, the magistrate added that whether instructions regarding document retention or collection were privileged "is far from certain," but did not decide the issue in light of the conclusions he reached. 2007 WL 2852364, at *2, n.3.

were worded or to how they described the legal issues in this action, plaintiffs are entitled to know what kinds and categories of ESI eBay employees were instructed to preserve and collect, and what specific actions they were instructed to undertake to that end.

Id. at *2 (footnote omitted). *See also Capitano v Ford Motor Co.*, 15 Misc. 3d 561, 564, 2007 NY Misc. LEXIS 453, at *3 (N.Y. Sup. Ct., Feb. 26, 2007) ("suspension orders" issued by Ford's lawyers in connection with litigation that were disseminated to only those employees who dealt with Ford's record management program and stated that they were privileged and confidential are attorney-client privileged communications under New York law).

Litigation hold memoranda have been produced in litigation, of course. See, e.g., *Lockheed Martin Corp. v. L-3 Communications Corp.*, 2007 U.S. Dist. LEXIS 79572 (M.D. Fla. Oct. 25, 2007) (witness testified he did not receive the litigation hold memorandum that was quoted in the magistrate's opinion). However, parties that claim that document retention-related documents are privileged and then produce them in part should be mindful of subject-matter waiver.[2]

Rambus, Inc. v. Infineon Technologies AG, 220 F.R.D. 264 (E.D. Va. 2004) illustrates the point. It is one of a trilogy of decisions related to Rambus's planned patent infringement litigation against several defendants and the prefiling designed destruction of documents.[3] Rambus had voluntarily produced some document retention-related documents but sought to protect others. That prompted Infineon to move to compel production

---

[2] A voluntary disclosure of privileged information may also require the production of all documents directly related to the same subject matter. See, e.g., In re Grand Jury Proceedings, 78 F.3d 251, 255–56, (6th Cir. 1996) (evaluating testimony that was the basis of the subject-matter waiver claim with respect to a marketing plan, and concluding that "prudential distinctions between what was revealed and what remains privileged" could be made: "Accordingly, we reverse the District Court's order to the extent it allows the government to ask the attorney unlimited questions about her advice on the entire marketing plan. Instead, the government may ask questions that clearly pertain to the subject matter of the specific points on which a waiver did occur.").

[3] See also Hynix Semiconductor, Inc. v. Rambus Inc., 2006 U.S. Dist. LEXIS 30690 (N.D. Cal. Jan. 4, 2006) (rejecting Hynix's unclean-hands defense to the patent infringement claim in part because it was not shown that Rambus adopted its document retention policy in bad faith); Samsung v. Rambus, Inc., 439 F. Supp. 2d 524 (E.D. Va. 2006) (on a motion for attorney fees brought by Samsung under 28 U.S.C. §285 or the court's inherent power, disagreeing with *Hynix*, but refusing to award fees in part because Samsung initiated the declaratory judgment action to establish an unclean-hands defense to claims of infringement, and Rambus had voluntarily dismissed its infringement counterclaims with prejudice).

of the withheld documents on the basis of subject-matter waiver.[4] The district court held that all claims of privilege with respect to all of Rambus's document retention–related documents likely had been waived, but withheld a final determination until after an *in camera* inspection of the documents. *Id.* at 290.[5]

One court looked at the terms of Rule 26(b)(1) in allowing discovery of document retention–related documents. In *Doe et al. v. District of Columbia*, 230 F.R.D. 47 (D.D.C. 2005), plaintiff sought in a Rule 30(b)(6) deposition, "testimony regarding '[t]he District's document retention policies and procedures, and the process used to collect the documents that have been produced or will be produced by the District in response to plaintiff's requests for production of documents.'" *Id.* at 55. Defendant argued that the request "violates the deliberative process and attorney-client privileges." Plaintiff responded by saying that "he wants to know only to what extent defendant is meeting its discovery obligations." *Id.* Without addressing the privilege claim or the scope of the questions that would be permitted of the Rule 30(b)(6) witness, the magistrate judge held that Rule 26(b)(1) may be construed to allow for discovery of document-production policies and procedures because it provides that parties can obtain discovery regarding any matter "including the existence, description, nature, custody, condition, and location of any... documents." The magistrate concluded: "Plaintiff may, therefore, request information as to the 'existence,' 'custody,' or 'condition' of documents,

---

[4] Infineon argued that because Rambus had voluntarily disclosed the substantive components of its document retention policy, Rambus had to disclose any related documents that would otherwise be protected by the attorney-client privilege under the subject-matter waiver rule. 220 F.R.D. at 288.

[5] The district court reviewed the case law on subject-matter waiver, saying that the cases suggested that "Rambus has waived the attorney client privilege as to any documents that contain information about or relate to the creation, preparation, or scope of its document retention policy, and, perhaps, even as to any documents that pertain to Rambus' patent litigation strategy." *Id.* at 289. The waiver had the potential to be extensive and might relate to the advice it received from counsel on the scope of the document retention policy. *Id.* "Having allowed testimony about the reasons for creating the document retention program and how it was implemented, it is arguable that Rambus cannot, under claims of privilege, restrict access to documents that address those topics. It, however, is appropriate to complete an *in camera* review of the privileged documents before deciding the issue of waiver." *Id.* at 290. Ultimately, the implementation of the prefiling document retention policy was found to have resulted in spoliation of evidence at a time when a duty to preserve existed. See Samsung v. Rambus, Inc., *supra,* 439 F. Supp. 2d at 527–28 (discussing decision in *Infineon* sustaining Infineon's unclean-hands defense to patent infringement claims brought by Rambus based on spoliation of evidence by Rambus).

thereby establishing defendant's policies and procedures of document retention and production." *Id.* at 56. Presumably, the deposition occurred and privilege objections were made to some questions, but, like the holding in *eBay*, plaintiff was entitled to know what defendant's employees did to collect documents to respond to plaintiff's discovery requests.[6]

Unilateral keyword searches reflecting counsel's thought processes are privileged. *Burroughs Wellcome Co. v. Barr Laboratories, Inc.*, 143 F.R.D. 611 (E.D.N.C. 1992), involved the assertion of the work-product privilege for the printed results of database searches conducted at the request of plaintiff's counsel. Plaintiff acknowledged that documents in the database were not privileged, but that the compilation of documents reflected "the attorney's legal theory and thought processes." The district court agreed with plaintiff: "The court agrees with plaintiff that the compilation of search results reflects the legal strategy of counsel. The court also finds that the searches were conducted in anticipation of litigation." *Id.* at 624. *See also Lockheed Martin Corp. v. L-3 Communications Corp.*, 2007 WL 2209250, at *10 (M.D. Fla. July 29, 2007) (documents "containing instructions about how to conduct the search and what specifically to search for are opinion work product").

On the other hand, ignoring one's opponent in identifying keyword searches may not comport with the spirit of Rule 26(f) and may incur the wrath of a judge, especially if the search is ill-conceived or faulty. *In re Seroquel Products Liability Litigation*, 2007 U.S. Dist. LEXIS 61287, at *39–40 (M.D. Fla. Aug. 21, 2007), is illustrative. The magistrate was critical of defendant's (AZ's) unilateral keyword search: "The key word search was plainly inadequate. Attachments, including nonverbal files, were not provided. Relevant e-mails were omitted." *Id.* at *39–40. The magistrate judge said the keyword search process should have been cooperative, not unilateral: "[W]hile key word searching is a recognized method to winnow relevant documents from large repositories, use of this technique must be a cooperative and informed process. Rather than working with Plaintiffs from the outset to reach agreement on appropriate and comprehensive search terms and methods, AZ undertook the task in secret." *Id.* at *41. The magistrate judge later repeated his conclusion saying that the Federal Rules require dialogue between counsel on search terms: "In this case, AZ never discussed with Plaintiffs which search terms to use

---

[6] I do not discuss document retention policies here. They may be privileged, but they would not be regarded as relevant in most matters. See, e.g., India Brewing Inc. v. Miller Brewing Co., 237 F.R.D. 190, 192 (E.D. Wis. 2006) (denying motion to compel production of document-retention policy on relevance grounds).

as part of the search. There was no dialogue to discuss the search terms, as required by Rules 26 and 34." *Id.* at *49.

And one court chastised the requesting party for failing to agree with the producing party on search terms, but then chastised the producing party for failing to conduct a unilateral search in the absence of an agreement:

> When it received the request, Biovail suggested defining the scope of any review of electronic records by stipulating which files would be searched and what search terms would be utilized. The plaintiff declined, apparently believing that "the use of search terms has no application to the standard discovery process of locating and producing accessible hard copy and electronic documents." The plaintiff's assumption is flawed....
>
> Yet the plaintiff's recalcitrance does not excuse Biovail's failure to produce any responsive documents whatsoever. Biovail suggested a strategy by which it would search the computer files of Mr. Melnyk, Mr. Cancellara, and Kenneth Howling, its director of investor relations, using the search terms: (i) Treppel, (ii) Jerry, (iii) Bank of America, (iv) Banc of America, (v) BAS, and (vi) BofA. Absent agreement with Mr. Treppel about a search strategy, Biovail should have proceeded unilaterally, producing all responsive documents located by its search. It shall now do so promptly. In addition, Biovail shall provide the plaintiff with a detailed explanation of the search protocol it implements.

Treppel v. Biovail Corp. et al., 233 F.R.D. 363, 374 (S.D.N.Y. 2006) (record references omitted). *Cf. O'Bar v. Lowe's Home Centers, Inc.*, 2007 U.S. Dist. LEXIS 32497, at *19 (W.D.N.C. May 2, 2007) (in offering guidelines to the parties on how to conduct e-discovery,[7] discussing search guidelines including "the use of key word searches, with an agreement on the words or terms to be searched"); *Balboa Threadworks, Inc. v. Stucky*, 2006 WL 763668, at *5 (D. Kan. Mar. 24, 2006) (directing parties to confer on a search protocol, "whether one using key word searches and/or other search procedures").

---

[7] The district court's *sua sponte* guidelines were based on "Suggested Protocol for Discovery of Electronically Stored Information" set forth by the United States District Court for the District of Maryland (available at www.mdd.uscourts.gov/news/news/ESIProtocol.pdf). Including the District of Maryland, there are thirty-two federal district courts that have adopted local "electronically stored information" discovery rules, protocols, or guidelines. Links to them can be found at www.ediscoverylaw.com/2007/10/articles/resources/updated-list-local-rules-of-united-states-district-courts-addressing-ediscovery-issues/.

Like all things e-discovery related, these keyword search cases emphasize cooperation, with the expectation that both the requesting party and the producing party are going to embody Rule 1's goal of a just, speedy, and inexpensive resolution of every issue in dispute. Where one side seeks to gain advantage or makes unreasonable demands or proposals, courts must step in and learn enough about the claims to ensure that the process is fair to both the requester and the producer without jeopardizing the work product of either.

CHAPTER THIRTEEN

Concept Searches: Has the Day Arrived for Computers to Replace Lawyers?

It does not pay to ignore the duty to preserve. *Disability Rights Council of Greater Wash. v. Wash. Metro. Transit Auth. (WMATA)*, 242 F.R.D. 139 (D.D.C. 2007), involved a claim by disabled persons that the WMATA violated the Americans with Disabilities Act and other federal laws. Suit was filed on March 25, 2004. The WMATA used Groupwise for e-mail, and the program automatically deleted all nonarchived e-mail every sixty days. Unfortunately for the WMATA, it failed to suspend its e-mail deletion program until, at the earliest, June 2006, more than two years after the complaint was filed. *Id.* at 145. The WMATA acknowledged the failure, which permitted the magistrate judge to conclude easily that defendant's failure to suspend the routine destruction of e-mail was "indefensible." *Id.* at 146.

Plaintiffs sought the restoration and review of backup tapes to find relevant e-mail deleted since the filing of the complaint. Defendants resisted the request, arguing that the backup tapes were not reasonably accessible. *Id.* at 147. Applying the balancing test in Rule 26(b)(2)(C), the magistrate judge found good cause to support plaintiffs' request. *Id.* at 148. Specifically, the magistrate judge determined that the benefit of production comfortably outweighed any burden to the WMATA because, among other reasons, there was no other place to find the documents due to the WMATA's failure to impose a litigation hold, the discovery was important to the outcome of the case, and plaintiffs had no meaningful financial resources. *Id.* at 148. The magistrate judge then ordered the restoration and search of the backup tapes according to a protocol that the parties were directed to negotiate. In so doing, the magistrate judge became the first court in the United States to suggest the possible use of "concept searching" as opposed to keyword searching. *Id.*[1]

Concept searching is broader than keyword searching:

> These more advanced text mining tools include "conceptual search methods" which rely on semantic relations between words, and/or which use "thesauri" to capture documents that would be missed in keyword searching....
>
> "Concept" search and retrieval technologies attempt to locate information that relates to a desired concept, without the presence of a particular word or phrase. The classic example is the concept search that will recognize that documents about Eskimos and igloos are related to Alaska, even if they do not specifically mention the word "Alaska."

"The Sedona Conference Best Practices Commentary on the Use and Information Retrieval Methods of E-Discovery," *2007 Sedona Conference Journal* 189, 202 (August 2007).[2]

Concept searches are an alternative to human review. They involve the use of "taxonomies"[3] and "ontologies"[4] applied to electronically stored

---

[1] "Once restored, how will they be searched to reduce the electronically stored information to information that is potentially relevant? In this context, I bring to the parties' attention recent scholarship that argues that concept searching, as opposed to keyword searching, is more efficient and more likely to produce the most comprehensive results. *See* George L. Paul & Jason R. Baron, *Information Inflation: Can the Legal System Adapt?*, 13 Rich. J.L. & Tech. 10 (2007)." 242 F.R.D. at 148.

[2] www.thesedonaconference.org/dltForm?did=Best_Practices_Retrieval_Methods___revised_cover_and_preface.pdf.

[3] "Taxonomy is a hierarchical scheme for representing classes and subclasses of concepts." 2007 Sedona Conference Journal at 221. If one's search category is "law personnel," then any document that mentions lawyer, paralegal, legal assistant, "esq.," or attorney would be picked up in the concept search. *Id.*

[4] "An ontology is a more generic species of taxonomy, often including a wider variety of relationship types than are found in the typical taxonomy. An ontology specifies the relevant set of conceptual categories and how they are related to one another." 2007

information to identify documents for production. Or they might rely "on mathematical probabilities that a certain text is associated with a particular conceptual category." *Id.* at 203.[5] The former rely on "information that linguists collect from the lawyers and witnesses about the key factual issues in the case the people, organization, and key concepts relating to the business as well as the idiosyncratic communications that might be lurking in documents, files, and e-mails." *Id.* The latter are "machine learning tools" and "are arguably helpful in addressing cultural biases of taxonomies because they do not depend on linguistic analysis, but on mathematical probabilities." *Id.*[6]

Keyword searches produce a universe of documents that have duplicates removed[7] and then are reviewed document by document with human eyes to determine responsiveness to a request for production. In their purest sense, once the design of search is completed, concept searches collapse these two steps into one.

The wholesale adoption of concept searching in litigation generally is not imminent. To develop the concept search requires a team of individuals who understand enough about the case to design relationships between words to ensure that the production is as good as or better than a human review. There is an expense associated with such an effort. Smaller dollar cases would not likely warrant such expenditure. In big dollar cases, concept searches would be intended to eliminate or reduce the cost of human review. Requesting parties may be skeptical that the approach will be substantively effective. They may request a parallel

---

SEDONA CONFERENCE JOURNAL at 222. To illustrate, if your search category includes "attorneys" then "you may also be interested in documents that use words such as 'lawyer,' 'paralegal,' or 'Esq.'" *Id.*

[5] "The simplest of these is the use of 'statistical clustering.' Clustering is the process of grouping together documents with similar content. There are a variety of ways to define similarity, but one way is to count the number of words that overlap between each pair of documents. The more words they have in common, the more likely they are to be about the same thing." *Id.* at 219.

[6] "They can also help to find communications in code language and neologisms. For example, if the labor lawyer were searching for evidence that management was targeting neophytes in the union, she might miss the term "n00b" (a neologism for "newbie"). This technology, used in government intelligence, is particularly apt in helping lawyers find information when they don't know exactly what to look for. For example, when a lawyer is looking for evidence that key players conspired to violate the labor union laws, she will usually not know the "code words" or expressions the players may have used to disguise their communications." *Id.* at 203.

[7] In small productions, the duplicates may not be removed to save cost. In large productions, deduping can be a time-consuming, difficult, and expensive process.

human effort to evaluate the thoroughness of the concept search before accepting it as a search protocol. Unless they can already demonstrate the effectiveness of a concept search, producing parties may not wish to expend the funds to prove the worth of concept searches.[8]

On the other hand, litigation is not disappearing in America; the volume of electronically stored information will continue to grow; e-discovery rules are in effect; and the cost of human review of huge volumes of information is enormous.[9] Hence, software advances and the refinement and acceptance of alternative search protocols in appropriate cases are developments lawyers should monitor.[10]

---

[8] One need not be too intuitive to conclude that the larger the document pool, and therefore the larger the potential cost savings, the more interested a document manager will be in concept searching. Hence, large corporations and government entities like the National Archives are at the forefront of experimenting with, and evaluating the effectiveness of, concept searching. For a slide presentation on a recent experiment with a vendor (H5) in which the conclusion was that the technological review was more effective than the human review, see www.h5technologies.com/news/webcasts.html. A pool of 48,000 documents was used in the experiment. There was no discussion of the cost involved.

[9] "In 1990, a typical gigabyte of storage cost about $20,000; today it costs less than $1 dollar [*sic*]. As a result, more individuals and companies are generating, receiving and storing more data, which means more information must be gathered, considered, reviewed and produced in litigation. But, with billable rates for junior associates at many law firms now starting at over $200 per hour, the cost to review just one gigabyte of data can easily exceed $30,000. These economic realities—*i.e.*, the huge cost differential between the $1 to store a gigabyte of data and the $30,000 to review it—act as a driver in changing the traditional attitudes and approaches of lawyers, clients, courts and litigation support providers about how to search for relevant evidence during discovery and investigations. Escalating data volumes into the billions of ESI objects, review costs, and shrinking discovery timetables, all add up to equaling the need for profound change." 2007 SEDONA CONFERENCE JOURNAL at 192. In a footnote, the authors explain that one gigabyte represents 70,000 to 80,000 pages, or 35 to 40 bankers' boxes at 2,000 pages to a box. A 100-gigabyte hard drive would thus hold 350 to 400 bankers' boxes of documents. *Id.*, n.2.

[10] Cf. Victor Stanley, Inc. v. Creative Pipe, Inc., 2008 WL 2221841, *5, n. 10 (D. Md. May 29, 2008) ("when parties decide to use a particular ESI search and retrieval methodology, they need to be aware of literature describing the strengths and weaknesses of various methodologies, such as *The Sedona Conference Best Practices, supra, n. 9*, and select the one that they believe is most appropriate for its intended task. Should their selection be challenged by their adversary, and the court be called upon to make a ruling, then they should expect to support their position with affidavits or other equivalent information from persons with the requisite qualifications and experience, based on sufficient facts or data and using reliable principles or methodology.") The magistrate was referring to the August 2007 Sedona Conference Best Practices Commentary cited in the text.

CHAPTER FOURTEEN

Metadata Searches: Is "Particularized Need" the New Standard?

The *Sedona Glossary*[1] defines metadata as:

> Data typically stored electronically that describes characteristics of ESI, found in different places in different forms. Can be supplied by applications, users or the file system. Metadata can describe how, when and by whom ESI was collected, created, accessed, modified and how it is formatted. Can be altered intentionally or inadvertently. Certain metadata can be extracted when native files are processed for litigation. Some metadata, such as file dates and sizes, can easily be seen by users; other metadata can be hidden or embedded and unavailable to computer users who are not technically adept. Metadata is generally not reproduced in full form when a document is printed to paper or electronic image.

---

[1] www.sedonaconference.org/dltForm?did=TSCGlossary_12_07.pdf (p. 33) (December 2007). There are different forms of metadata. The *Sedona Glossary* contains definitions for Application Metadata, Document Metadata, E-mail Metadata, Embedded Metadata, File System Metadata, User-Added Metadata, and Vendor-Added Metadata. *Id.* A request for "all metadata" would be *ipso facto* overbroad.

A pocket guide provided to federal judges by the United States Judicial Conference gives this definition of metadata:

> Metadata, which most computer users never see, provide information about an electronic file, such as the date it was created, its author, when and by whom it was edited, what edits were made, and, in the case of e-mail, the history of its transmission.[2]

Yet another description appears in *Williams v. Sprint/United Mgmt. Co.*, 230 F.R.D. 640, 646 (D. Kan. 2005) (footnotes omitted):

> Some examples of metadata for electronic documents include: a file's name, a file's location (e.g., directory structure or pathname), file format or file type, file size, file dates (e.g., creation date, date of last data modification, date of last data access, and date of last metadata modification), and file permissions (e.g., who can read the data, who can write to it, who can run it). Some metadata, such as file dates and sizes, can easily be seen by users; other metadata can be hidden or embedded and unavailable to computer users who are not technically adept.

The case law is mixed and is intertwined with the issue of the form of production. For example, in *Williams v. Sprint/United Management Company, supra*, the magistrate judge held that production in native format means that metadata must also be produced unless objection is made. Despite explaining that "[e]merging standards of electronic discovery appear to articulate a general presumption against the production of metadata," *id.* at 651, the magistrate judge held: "When the Court orders a party to produce an electronic document in the form in which it is regularly maintained, i.e., in its native format or as an active file, that production must include all metadata unless that party timely objects to production of the metadata, the parties agree that the metadata should not be produced, or the producing party requests a protective order."[3] *See*

---

[2] Managing Discovery of Electronic Information: A Pocket Guide for Judges (2007), p. 3, www.uscourts.gov/rules/eldscpkt.pdf.

[3] In a later opinion, the same magistrate judge refused to require production of metadata for certain electronically stored information where the requesting party could not justify a need for it. Williams v. Sprint/United Management Co., 2006 WL 3691604, at *14 (D. Kan. Dec. 12, 2006): "Previously, this Court has ordered Defendant to produce the Excel RIF spreadsheets in native format, but in that instance Plaintiffs provided valid reasons for the spreadsheets to be produced in their native format. Namely, that the contents of the spreadsheet cells could not otherwise be viewed as the cells contained formulas. Also, in many instances, the column width of the cells prevented viewing of the entire content of

also Nova Measuring Instruments LTD. v. Nanometrics, Inc., 417 F. Supp. 2d 1121, 1122 (N.D. Cal. 2006) (requiring production in native format "with original metadata"). There are opinions on the other side of this issue.

Wyeth v. Impax Labs, 2006 U.S. Dist. LEXIS 79761 (D. Del. Oct. 26, 2006), seized on the presumption in *Williams*, not the holding. Defendant in this patent dispute sought an order compelling Wyeth to produce its electronic documents "in their native format, complete with metadata, and not in the Tagged Image File Format ('TIFF') in which they were produced." *Id.* at *3. Plaintiff responded that defendant was not entitled to the electronic copies in their native form because defendant had not made a "particularized showing of need" for the data and the collection of the data in this format would be "overly burdensome." *Id.* at *4–5. The district court denied defendant's request to compel production, relying, in part, on *Williams*. The district court ultimately ruled that because the parties had not agreed in advance how the electronic documents were to be produced, Wyeth had "complied with its discovery obligation by producing image files." *Id.* at *5. The district court also reasoned that Impax had not demonstrated a "particularized need for the metadata." *Id.*[4]

Kentucky Speedway, LLC v. Nat'l Assoc. of Stock Car Auto Racing, Inc., 2006 U.S. Dist. LEXIS 92028 (E.D. Ky. Dec. 18, 2006), piggybacked on *Wyeth*. In this antitrust case, plaintiff sought metadata for all of the records that

---

the cells. Here, other than arguing that ordering Defendant to reproduce the transmittal e-mails together with their attachments in native format would be more helpful to Plaintiffs in matching up the transmittal e-mails with their respective attachments, Plaintiffs fail to provide any other reason why they need the transmittal e-mails produced in their native format. For these reasons, the Court denies Plaintiffs' request for Defendant to produce all its RIF-related transmittal e-mails in native format with all attachments in native format and attached to the transmittal e-mails."

[4] The United States District Court for the District of Delaware has adopted default standards for e-discovery that are applicable where the parties cannot agree on e-discovery issues. For the "Format" of production, the Delaware District Court default standards provide that, in the absence of agreement, metadata must be preserved but need not be produced unless a "particularized need" is shown. Default Standard 6 (D. Del.) provides: "If, during the course of the Rule 26(f) conference, the parties cannot agree to the format for production of their electronically stored information, as permitted by Fed. R. Civ. P. 34, such information shall be produced to the requesting party as text searchable image files (e.g., PDF or TIFF), unless unduly burdensome or cost-prohibitive to do so. When a text searchable image file is produced, the producing party must preserve the integrity of the underlying electronically stored information, i.e., the original formatting, the metadata and, where applicable, the revision history. After initial production in text searchable image file format is complete, a party must demonstrate particularized need for production of electronically stored information in native format." The default standards can be found at www.ded.uscourts.gov/Announce/Policies/Policy01.htm.

were electronically produced in the case up to that point. *Id.* at *21. The district court explicitly rejected the holding in *Williams*, finding its conclusion that a producing party should produce its electronic data with the metadata intact unpersuasive. *Id.* at *22. Instead the district court relied on *Wyeth*. The district court determined that because plaintiff did not show a "particularized need," and because the metadata would not have necessarily identified a document's author, the metadata was not necessarily relevant to the case. *Id.* at *23–24. The district court added that "[t]o the extent that plaintiff seeks metadata for a specific document or documents where date and authorship information is unknown but relevant, plaintiff should identify that document or documents by Bates Number or by other reasonably identifying features." *Id.* at *24.

Celerity v. Ultra Clean Holding, Inc. et al., 2007 U.S. Dist. LEXIS 18307, (N.D. Cal. Feb. 28, 2007), was a patent infringement case in which the defendant was relying on outside counsel's opinion of noninfringement as a defense to plaintiff's claim. Defendant had produced billing records with entries showing that there had been multiple revisions to the opinion. Defendant, however, had produced only the final version. It explained that the author overwrote the older drafts in the process of writing the final version. That prompted the plaintiff to ask for "metadata which would reflect these earlier drafts." The magistrate judge ruled that defendant should produce the metadata, and if the metadata did not exist, "a sworn declaration to that effect shall be filed." *Id.* at **9.

The magistrate judge in *Michigan First Credit Union v. Cumis Insurance Society, Inc.*, 2007 WL 4098213 (E.D. Mich. Nov. 16, 2007) concluded that metadata need not be produced. Three types of electronically stored information were involved. With regard to the first type, no metadata was created by the software in question. So the magistrate judge concluded that the issue of metadata production was "moot." "Defendant cannot produce what does not exist." *Id.* at *2. With regard to Lotus Notes e-mail messages, the magistrate accepted the testimony of defendant's witness that all metadata generated appeared in the printed version of the e-mails. "Were this not the case, there would be value in producing the metadata. However, since the PDF copies contain all the relevant information that Plaintiff would otherwise glean from the metadata, I agree with Defendant that producing the metadata for the e-mails would be unduly burdensome." *Id.* Finally, as to Microsoft Office documents, defendant's witness said the documents were kept in paper form in the regular course of business and producing metadata would consume substantial resources. The magistrate refused to require production of the metadata: "Given the admonitions of *Williams v. Sprint*, *Wyeth*, and

Kentucky Speedway, supra, regarding the relative lack of worth of metadata, and the lack of any showing by Plaintiff that the metadata underlying Microsoft Office documents would be likely to lead to the discovery of relevant evidence, I agree with Defendant that the production of this metadata would be overly burdensome with no corresponding evidentiary value." *Id.* at *3.

Litigation in the United States has occurred for more than two hundred years without metadata. Trends are not easy to predict in the e-discovery field, but if I had to predict one, it would be that in most cases, metadata will not be sought or ordered produced unless there is a particularized need demonstrated by the requesting party.

CHAPTER FIFTEEN

Does One Form of Production Really Mean Just One Form?

Restyled Rule 34(b)(2)(E) provides that "unless otherwise stipulated or ordered by the court, these procedures apply to producing documents or electronically stored information":

> (i) A party must produce documents as they are kept in the usual course of business or must organize and label them to correspond to the categories in the request;
>
> (ii) If a request does not specify a form for producing electronically stored information, a party must produce it in a form or forms in which it is ordinarily maintained or in a reasonably usable form or forms; and
>
> (iii) A party need not produce the same electronically stored information in more than one form.

In the case of electronically stored information, does subparagraph (ii) trump (iii)?

In *The Scotts Co. LLC v. Liberty Mutual Ins. Co.*, 2007 U.S. Dist. LEXIS 43005 (S.D. Ohio June 12, 2007), defendant had produced paper copies of electronically stored information because the requesting party had not specified a form. Plaintiff requested reproduction in electronic form because defendant had an obligation under Rule 34 to produce documents in a "reasonably usable form." Defendant said it was not obligated to produce documents in more than one form. Instead of ruling on the request, the magistrate ordered the parties to confer, but arguably signaled the outcome:

> Indeed, the Advisory Committee explains, "If the responding party ordinarily maintains the information it is producing in a way that makes it searchable by electronic means, the information should not be produced in a form that removes or significantly degrades this feature." Plaintiff now argues that some of the documents produced in hard copy form are not reasonably usable for the purpose for which they were requested since they cannot be searched for metadata.
>
> It is unclear to this Court whether the parties have fully exhausted extra-judicial efforts to resolve this dispute. The parties are therefore ORDERED to meet and confer within ten days with regard to this issue.

Id. at *14–15 (emphasis in original).

In *3M Company v. Kanbar et al.*, 2007 U.S. Dist. LEXIS 45232 (N.D. Cal. June 14, 2007), Kanbar made broad production requests but failed to request documents in electronic format. Paper documents were produced. Kanbar had insufficient staff to process the paper production. So it moved to compel 3M to "organize" or "itemize" the documents that had been produced. The motion was denied. However, because it appeared that 3M to some extent delayed its production and because it was not onerous for 3M to do so, the magistrate judge gave the defendant relief: He ordered 3M "to produce all previously produced responsive electronically stored information" in an electronic and "reasonably usable format." *Id.* at *9–10. "Although the electronic production does not provide Kanbar quite what it asked for, this order should enable Defendant to utilize commercially available software search engines to accomplish by its own undertaking at least some of what it unsuccessfully sought from the Court." *Id.* at *10.

In *PSEG Power New York Inc. v. Alberici Constructors*, 2007 U.S. Dist. LEXIS 66767 (N.D.N.Y. Sept. 7, 2007), PSEG provided e-mails and their respective attachments in hard copy. Alberici wanted them in electronic form. PSEG balked because of the estimated cost of $200,000. Alberici scoffed at this estimate, saying it found a vendor who would charge $37,500 for the work. After noting Rule 34(b)(2)(E)(iii)'s prescription that a producing party need only produce documents in one form, the magistrate explained that the production "was made in contravention of Rule 34's direction to produce the information as kept in the original course of business and in a form that is reasonably usable," that is, under Rule 34(b)(2)(E)(i) and (ii). *Id.* at *26–27. The inability of PSEG's vendor to produce the e-mails with their associated attachments caused the problem in the first instance. Hence, the magistrate ordered PSEG to produce 3,000 e-mails and their attachments at its expense, but not without a number of options.

> In the final analysis, based upon the reasons stated above, the burden of production and the assumption of the cost remains with the responding party, PSEG. The burden is being placed upon the party who will decide the extent of the expense. But we are prepared to give PSEG some options in order to meet their re-production obligation. If PSEG does not want to assume the computer generated, re-production process, then PSEG may review the entire mass production of 2006, which was done in hard copy, and identify the attachments for each e-mail for Alberici. Whether this identification process entails re-producing them in hard copy or creating another specific spreadsheet for this purpose, either would suffice. To the extent that some of the e-mails may be a duplication of others since they have been circulated throughout the agency, as many e-mails are, PSEG may identify those e-mails as duplication of others which would obviate the need to re-produce them. If working with hard copies is not acceptable, then PSEG will have to access the PST files on its own and bear the cost, whatever that may be. Nonetheless, we suggest if PSEG pursues this approach it should employ Alberici's vendor whose cost was one-fifth of PSEG's vendor. If this method is pursued, PSEG should enter into a contract with strict rules of engagement and confidentiality provisions that would protect its privileged, confidential, and proprietary information. If required, the Court is prepared to issue a protective order to lend all of the protection necessary to fulfill PSEG's needs. *Rowe Entm't Inc. v. William Morris Agency Inc.*, 205 F.R.D. at 428 ("To the extent that the corporate defendants' own privacy interest[s] are at issue, they are adequately protected by [a] confidentiality order[.]"). Or, PSEG can find another vendor who would be able to extract this information at a cost far less than $200,000, which we submit can be done without further fanfare or knottiness. Or, if PSEG has found another mechanism to re-produce these e-mails at a cost savings, exclusive of requiring Alberici to expend considerable time and resources,

we invite it to do so. All other options aside, it seems that using Alberici's vendor would be most prudent but the choice of vendors to extract the information and complete the e-mail distribution rests with PSEG.

Id. at *34–36.

Puckett v. Tandem Staffing Solutions, Inc. 2007 U.S. Dist. LEXIS 47287 (N.D. Ill. June 27, 2007), is yet another case where the way a party maintained documents in the "usual course of business" became outcome determinative.

Puckett complained that Tandem produced documents from only ten of thirty-four backup tapes and refused to produce backup tapes that contained electronic documents other than e-mails. *Id.* at *7. With respect to the e-mail backup tapes, Tandem explained that its third-party vendor "found that several of the tapes were unrestorable after several attempts to restore them, several tapes had file mark errors, and several tapes did not contain relevant information." *Id.* at *7–8. The district court found this response to be sufficient and required no further response by Tandem. *Id.* at *8.

However, with respect to backup tapes containing documents, Tandem argued that it had not restored them "because it has produced these multiple documents in hard copy other than attachments as e-mails." The district court ordered production in electronic format anyway:

As this information is reasonably calculated to lead to the discovery of admissible evidence, this Court believes that restoration of the back-up tapes containing documents is reasonable. Tandem has asserted that in its usual course of business it maintains its documentation in an electronic format. The Court will limit this request to production of the back-up tapes of documents saved to the network system from September 2004 until September 2005.

Id. at *8. The district court, did, however, without discussion, order Puckett to pay 50 percent of the cost of restoration of these backup tapes. *Id.* at *11–12.

In *Lawson v. Sun Microsystems, Inc.,* 2007 U.S. Dist. LEXIS 65530 (S.D. Ind. Sept. 4, 2007), plaintiff, in a letter dated January 17, 2007, requested production in an electronic format. Plaintiff then served its first request for production on April 5, 2007, but did not again specify the form of production. Defendant produced documents in hard copy on May 8, 2007. In a motion to compel, plaintiff sought electronic versions of the documents. Defendant objected, saying it was obligated to produce only in one form. The magistrate judge ordered the production, saying that the letter sent in January provided sufficient notice of the form of production sought by plaintiff. *Id.* at *13. The magistrate added:

> Defendant has not indicated to the Court that it objected to Plaintiff's format request before proceeding to produce documents to Plaintiff in a format contrary to that requested by Plaintiff. Furthermore, Defendant has provided no reason for not producing the electronically stored documents in electronic format other than inconvenience and Defendant's mistaken belief that Plaintiff's format request came after Defendant had begun production. Therefore, Defendant shall produce to Plaintiff all electronically stored information in electronic format.

Id. at *13–14.

There are, of course, decisions where a producing party was not required to produce in electronic format documents that had been produced in hard copy. See, e.g., *India Brewing, Inc. v. Miller Brewing Co.*, 237 F.R.D. 190, 194–95 (E.D. Wisc. 2006) (where plaintiff did not specify a form of production, plaintiff was not entitled to production in electronic format where electronic documents were produced in hard copy to correspond to discovery requests); *Northern Crossarm Co. Inc. v. Chemical Specialties, Inc.*, 2004 WL 635606 (W.D. Wis. March 3, 2004) (where plaintiff did not specify the form of production, defendant produced in hard copy, and there was no gamesmanship involved, request for production in electronic format was denied).

So does Rule 34(b)(2)(E)(ii) trump (iii)? As you can see from the above, the answer will be "at times, yes, and at times, no"; in other words, "sometimes."[1]

---

[1] This is another area where parties are well advised to take advantage of the Rule 26(f) meet-and-confer session and Rule 16 conference to achieve a consensus on how best to proceed and to avoid misunderstandings or miscommunication that could lead to later discovery disputes.

CHAPTER SIXTEEN

Should You Take a Consultant to the Rule 26 Meet-and-Confer Session?

Lawyers debate whether they should have e-discovery consultants present at the meet-and-confer session required under Rule 26(f). If a case merits the retention of an e-discovery consultant, chances are having the e-discovery consultant present, or at least nearby or easily accessible by telephone, may make sense.

The magistrate judge in *In re Seroquel Products Liability Litigation, supra,* expressed his upset with the decision of the defendant to shield its third-party contractor from the plaintiffs:

> Many of the other technical problems identified by [plaintiff's experts] likely could have been resolved far sooner and less expensively had AZ cooperated by fostering consultation between the technical staffs responsible for production. Instead, AZ shielded its third party technical contractor from all contact with Plaintiffs. This approach is antithetical to the Sedona Principles and is not an indicium of good faith.

2007 U.S. Dist. LEXIS 61287, at *41.

Lawyers involved in *Crown Park Corp. v. Dominican Sisters of Mary Mother of the Eucharist*, 2006 U.S. Dist. LEXIS 19739 (E.D. Mich. April 24,

2006), had no choice in the matter. Plaintiff had sought an *ex parte* preservation order, which was denied by the magistrate judge. The magistrate instead ordered each party to appear at the meet-and-confer with an electronic document consultant who had sufficient knowledge of each party's electronic documents to enable the parties to participate in "a good faith effort to resolve all issues regarding the production of electronic documents without court action." *Id.* at *3–4. The consultants were not to be subject to discovery without the district court's permission unless either side's consultant provided testimony on an issue, in which case discovery would have been limited to that issue. If the parties could not agree on a preservation plan, they were to submit to the magistrate judge for resolution a statement of unresolved issues together with each party's proposed resolution. *Id.* at 4.

The case law will continue to develop but where e-discovery consultants are retained, the likely emphasis of courts will be on taking advantage of them to educate, communicate, and collaborate within a framework of reasonableness to identify sensible, cost-effective solutions to legitimate e-discovery issues.[1]

---

[1] Cf. Equity Analytics v. Lundin, 248 FRD 331, 333 (D.D.C. 2008). Building on his opinion in United States v. O'Keefe, 2008 WL 44972, at *8 (D.D.C. Feb. 18, 2008) in which the magistrate judge questioned the expertise of lawyers to opine on the efficacy of search methodologies, the magistrate explained that "determining whether a particular search methodology, such as keywords, will or will not be effective certainly requires knowledge beyond the ken of a lay person (and a lay lawyer) and requires expert testimony that meets the requirements of Rule 702 of the Federal Rules of Evidence. Obviously, determining the significance of the loading of a new operating system upon file structure and retention and why the contemplated forensic search will yield information that will not be yielded by a search limited by file types or keywords are beyond any experience or knowledge I can claim." The magistrate then required the producing party to submit an affidavit from its forensic examiner to explain why certain limitations on discovery of his home computer proposed by the plaintiff were not likely to capture information sought by the discovery request, why the loading of a new operating system on plaintiff's McIntosh computer would alter data, and how the examiner proposed to conduct the search, after which the magistrate then would either rule or hold a hearing where cross examination would be permitted so that the magistrate could balance the requesting party's need for information against the producing party's privacy. See also Victor Stanley, Inc. v. Creative Pipe, Inc., 2008 WL 2221841, *5, n. 10 (D. Md. May 29, 2008) (parties objecting to search methodologies selected by their opponent should be expected to support their objections with affidavits or information from qualified individuals).

CHAPTER SEVENTEEN

A Different Form of Computer Monitor: How Do You Make Sure That a Party Complies with E-Discovery Obligations?

Ignoring a consent decree or court order requiring production of electronically stored information is unwise. Just ask Tennessee's public officials charged with caring for children. In *John B. v. Goetz*, 2007 WL 3012808 (M.D. Tenn. Oct. 10, 2007), a very displeased district court ordered defendant state agencies to produce responsive electronically stored information with all metadata and all deleted information on any computer of certain key custodians. The plaintiffs' expert was allowed to be present for the production and was permitted to inspect defendants' computer system "to assess whether any changes have been made to hinder the ESI production required by the Consent Decree or previously Ordered by the Court." *Id.* at *1. The district court also decided to appoint a monitor to ensure that discovery was completed in a satisfactory and timely manner. *Id.* The appointed monitor was given the authority to hire a computer expert and to communicate with the district court, in writing, regarding the progress of discovery. The district court further ordered the defendants to pay the costs of the monitor and any expert hired by the monitor because their conduct caused the discovery disputes. *Id.*

Discovery was also sought by the plaintiffs from a number of managed care contractors (MCCs). The district court required these third parties to produce electronically stored information based on search terms determined by the district court (with leave given to plaintiffs to renew a request to use their search terms if the production was "seriously inadequate"). *Id.* at *2. The district court also issued an order to show cause why the state agency defendants should not be required to pay the production costs of the MCCs, *including* their attorney's fees and costs. *Id.*

The district court subsequently issued orders dated November 15 and 19, 2007, authorizing the immediate forensic imaging of any computers used by fifty officials—at state offices or at their homes—whom the defendants designated as key custodians of materials responsive to discovery requests. The district court also issued opinions denying a motion for reconsideration, 2007 WL 4014015 (M.D. Tenn. Nov. 15, 2007) and a motion for stay pending appeal, 2007 WL 4198266 (Nov. 26, 2007).

Defendants filed a petition for writ of mandamus in the Sixth Circuit seeking relief from the discovery orders and arguing that an indiscriminate sweep of the state's computer systems would reveal privileged and confidential governmental information. The orders of the district court were stayed temporarily by the Sixth Circuit on the same date that the district court issued an opinion denying a stay request. *John B. v. Goetz*, No. 07-6373 (6th Cir. Nov. 26, 2007). After further considering the motion at a motions' panel conference, the Sixth Circuit stayed the district court's orders and expedited the briefing. *Id.* (Dec. 7, 2007). The states of Kentucky, Michigan, and Ohio filed amicus briefs in support of the position of the state of Tennessee.

On June 26, 2008, the Sixth Circuit granted the petition in part. *John B. v. Goetz*, ___ F.3d ___, 2008 WL 2520487 (6th Cir. 2008). For reasons of federalism and comity, and to protect against intrusions of privacy, the court of appeals vacated those portions of the district court's orders that permitted forensic imaging of all hard drives and other devices that contained relevant electronically stored information and that required federal marshals to accompany plaintiffs' computer expert in the execution of the orders. *Id.* at *6.

> [T]he mere imaging of the media, in and of itself, raises privacy and confidentiality concerns. Duplication, by its very nature, increases the risk of improper exposure, whether purposeful or inadvertent. Further, counsel for plaintiffs conceded at oral argument that the information contained on the hard drives, including information not related to this litigation, must eventually be accessed to determine relevance.
>
> As directives to state officials, these orders implicate federalism and comity considerations not present in typical civil litigation. Many of the computers subject to the orders are in the custody of high ranking state officials, and these computers will contain information related to confidential state matters. Further, the orders call for federal law enforcement officers to accompany plaintiffs' computer expert into state agencies--and, in some cases, the homes and offices of state officials--to effect the imaging. These procedures clearly do not take adequate account of federalism and comity considerations. If the use of federal law enforcement officers in matters of civil discovery is proper under some circumstances, those circumstances are not present here.

Id. at *7, 11.

The court of appeals added that, because "litigants are generally responsible for preserving relevant information on their own," forensic imaging of hard drives as a means to preserve electronically stored information, "if at all appropriate, should be employed in a very limited set of circumstances." Id. at *9. And then forensic imaging should only be permitted when there is an "interest significant enough to override the risk" that confidential state or private personal information "that is wholly unrelated to the litigation" will be revealed. *Id.* at *10. And because of these privacy concerns, the court of appeals advised the district court to look at other options first if it is unhappy with a state party's compliance with discovery obligations.

> Furthermore, forensic imaging is not the only available means by which the district court may respond to what it perceives to be discovery misconduct. The district court maintains authority to impose sanctions for discovery violations under the federal rules and pursuant to its inherent powers. Although we take no position regarding the propriety of sanctions in this case, such measures

99

can be less intrusive than forensic imaging, and it is not apparent from the record that the district court has exercised its sanctioning authority.

Id.

A pyrrhic victory? The State might have preferred to image the office hard drives itself to protect itself against accusations of spoliation, or to allow imaging but with a confidential information and privacy protection protocol, but these approaches were not apparently options that State elected to pursue. Instead, the computer monitor survived the mandamus order, and while the monitor won't have U.S. marshals accompanying him, the state still had to satisfy the monitor that it has met its obligations to preserve and produce relevant electronically stored information for all of the fifty key custodians on any storage media they used, with a risk of sanctions looming over the State if it fails to do so.

CHAPTER EIGHTEEN

Can You Use a Subpoena to Obtain Information from an Opposing Expert?

In *Auto Club Family Ins. Co. v. Ahner*, 2007 U.S. Dist. LEXIS 63809 (E.D. La. Aug. 29, 2007), a subpoena issuer sought documents in electronic form from a third-party engineering firm, Rimkus, that had investigated post–Hurricane Katrina insurance claims and was the expert for the defendant insurance company. Rimkus wanted to produce in paper because it mimicked Rimkus's electronic file and the client had been supplied with a paper copy. It argued that electronic production would "compromise the authenticity and integrity of its engineering reports," which it always provided in PDF format to preclude alteration of professional findings. *Id.* at *4–5.

However, there was no evidence provided by Rimkus to support its fear of alteration. The district court ordered production in electronic form. *Id.* at *5–6. The district court explained that the paper file "deliberately retained" by Rimkus was highly unlikely to contain all of the responsive material that was generated during its investigation. The type of information likely to be missing from the hard-copy file "may well include, for example, working papers, e-mails requesting clarification, rough drafts and similar materials that are neither incorporated in final reports nor, perhaps, deemed worthy of retention in hard copy." *Id.* at *6.[1]

The fact that Rimkus was the testifying expert for the defendant supported the outcome. *Id.* at *7. There is also no prohibition on serving a subpoena *duces tecum* on an opponent's expert, according to the magistrate. "Rule 26(b)(4) only restricts when a party may depose its opponent's testifying and non-testifying experts or propound interrogatories to its opponent's non-testifying experts; it does not limit document requests." *Id.* at *8.[2]

While the motion to quash the subpoena was denied,[3] the magistrate added that cost shifting might be appropriate if the proper showing were made:

> If [the subpoena recipient] can prove that responding to this subpoena imposes unreasonable burden or costs upon it as a non-party, it may file a new motion, supported by evidence, seeking to impose some or all of such costs upon the parties who issued the subpoena. Fed. R. Civ. P. 26(c)(2), 45(c).

Id. at. *16.[4]

---

[1] In April 2008, the Advisory Committee on the Federal Rules of Civil Procedure agreed to recommend to the Standing Committee on the rules, amendments to Rule 26(a) and (b) that would result in the treatment of draft expert reports as work product and that would extend work product protection to communications between counsel and experts except for those relating to compensation of the expert, those that identify facts or data that counsel provided to the expert, and those that identify assumptions provided to the expert by counsel and that the expert relied upon in framing an opinion. These changes, if adopted after public comment, would not likely effect until December 2010.

[2] Rule 26(b)(4)(A) provides: "A party may depose any person who has been identified as an expert whose opinions may be presented at trial." Rule 26(b)(4)(B) provides that consulting experts cannot be subjected to discovery "by interrogatories or deposition" with limited exceptions. Presumably, the parties did not have an agreement on the scope of production of draft opinions and other documents by each side's experts.

[3] Rimkus's other arguments failed as well. On the issue of the inaccessibility of the documents, the magistrate said there was a failure of proof: "The statement of a lawyer in a memorandum that the electronic information is not readily accessible or that it would be unduly burdensome to comply with the request is not evidence." 2007 U.S. Dist. LEXIS 63809, at *8–9. At oral argument, Rimkus then claimed work-product protection. The claim was rejected. A blanket assertion of privilege is not enough; there must be proof to substantiate the privilege claim, the magistrate held. *Id.* at *12–14.

[4] Restyled Rule 45(c)(2)(B)(i) and (ii) address the costs of responding to a subpoena when an order is issued compelling production: "(i) At any time, on notice to the commanded person, the serving party may move the issuing court for an order compelling production or inspection. (ii) These acts may be required only as directed in the order, and the order must protect a person who is neither a party nor a party's officer from significant expense resulting from compliance." See, e.g., Guy Chemical Co., Inc. v. Romaco AG et al., 2007 U.S. Dist. LEXIS 37636, at *7–8 (N.D. Ind. May 22, 2007) (ordering subpoena-issuer to pay the costs of production).

CHAPTER NINETEEN

Should Subpoena Issuers Have Their Checkbooks Ready?

Rule 45(c)(1) directs a party serving a subpoena to take "reasonable steps to avoid imposing undue burden or expense on a person subject to the subpoena." The Advisory Committee Note alerts the district courts to be vigilant in enforcing the protective provisions of Rule 45(c).[1] Given this warning, one would expect that issuers of subpoenas will tailor the breadth of the request so that important information is being sought that will not be cost-prohibitive for the nonparty to obtain, and the likelihood that information will be found, the availability of other sources of the evidence, the amount in controversy, and the burden of production will play prominent roles in whether the third-party subpoena recipient will even be required to respond.

Requesting parties who fail to heed this advice are not likely to receive much sympathy from a district court. In *Quinby v. Westlb AG*, 2006 U.S. Dist. LEXIS 1178, at *3 (S.D.N.Y. Jan. 11, 2006), the magistrate judge quashed subpoenas to Internet service providers for plaintiff's e-mails within a defined period of time because the subpoenas were "clearly

---

[1] www.uscourts.gov/rules/supct1105/Excerpt_CV_Report.pdf (p. 93).

overbroad." The subpoena recipient in *In re Natural Gas Commodity Litigation*, 2005 U.S. Dist. LEXIS 27470 (S.D.N.Y. Nov. 14, 2005), was a "small organization," and historical data sought by plaintiffs resided on "old" and "antiquated individual computers." Plaintiffs had wisely offered to pay for specially retained outside personnel to search the old computers and to pay for technical and clerical staff to be hired by the subpoena recipient to redact information not sought by the plaintiffs. The magistrate judge first required plaintiffs and the subpoena recipient to negotiate a reasonable "sample" protocol, "perhaps searching one of the 'old' computers, with leave to re-visit the burden versus utility question based on information from that process." *Id.* at *68–69.

An offer to pay the nonparty subpoena responder's cost of producing e-mails from backup tapes did not help the subpoena issuer in *United States, et al. v. Amerigroup Illinois Inc., et al.*, 2005 U.S. Dist. LEXIS 24929 (N.D. Ill. Oct. 21, 2005). The burden was still found to be "undue":

> It is not a decisive answer to say that the defendants have offered to pay the costs that might be incurred in retrieving the e-mails. Expense is but a part of the burden. As Mr. Petty's uncontested affidavit indicates, the process of retrieving the e-mails also entails the extensive use of equipment and internal man-power. It will take six weeks to restore and review the data of just one of the three individual's e-mail accounts. The entire project, then, will entail eighteen weeks of effort. To be sure, one can imagine the use of three dedicated servers to perform each of the six weeks of restoration work concurrently, but the end result is still eighteen weeks of man-power and eighteen weeks of use of the necessary equipment. That burden, which is undeniably substantial, exists independently of the monetary costs entailed.

Id. at *13. The defendants did not help their cause by claiming that the e-mails were critical to the "government knowledge" defense alleged in the case where, eleven months earlier, they had filed a motion for summary judgment saying that they should prevail on that defense based on the facts then in existence. *Id.* at *21–22.

The issue of legal fees has been raised in different contexts under Rule 45. In *Guy Chemical Co., Inc. v. Romaco AG et al.*, 2007 U.S. Dist. LEXIS 37636 (N.D. Ind. May 22, 2007), the magistrate denied a motion to compel and required payment to the third party of its costs of production under Rule 45(c)(2)(B)(ii) because the subpoena imposed an undue burden and cost upon the subpoena recipient. The magistrate refused to award attorneys' fees expended to respond to the motion because Rule 45 had just been amended, and the issue was a "novel" one. In *In re Automotive Refinishing Paint Antitrust Litigation*, 2005 U.S. Dist. LEXIS 22353 (E.D. Pa. June 29, 2005), plaintiffs requested numerous documents, including electronic files, from a nonparty international nonprofit trade organization with a staff of eight people. The magistrate determined that compliance would be "burdensome." Plaintiff was required to compensate the subpoena recipient for the costs of production, including legal fees.

Subpoena issuers who do not tailor their requests and show consideration of the burden and cost imposed on a subpoena recipient by a subpoena should expect to have to get out their checkbooks.

CHAPTER TWENTY

Are States Close Behind?

State court decisions or rules of procedure addressing electronic discovery will begin to arrive in the coming months and years, and they most likely will be patterned in whole or in part on the federal rules.

Illustratively, the Alabama Supreme Court determined that Fed. R. Civ. P. 26(b)(2)(C) and the *Wiginton* cost-shifting factors[1] should be used in considering the extent to which parties in Alabama state court actions must respond to discovery requests for electronically stored information. *Ex parte Cooper Tire & Rubber Co.*, 2007 Ala. LEXIS 229 (Ala. Oct. 26, 2007).[2] The Alabama Supreme Court gave this guidance to the trial court:

---

[1] Wiginton v. CB Richard Ellis, Inc., 229 F.R.D. 568, 571–73 (N.D. Ill. 2004). The magistrate judge modified the *Zubulake* factors by adding an eighth factor "that considers the importance of the requested discovery in resolving the issues of the litigation." He wrote: "Therefore, we will consider the following factors: 1) the likelihood of discovering critical information; 2) the availability of such information from other sources; 3) the amount in controversy as compared to the total cost of production; 4) the parties' resources as compared to the total cost of production; 5) the relative ability of each party to control costs and its incentive to do so; 6) the importance of the issues at stake in the litigation; 7) the importance of the requested discovery in resolving the issues at stake in the litigation; and 8) the relative benefits to the parties of obtaining the information. At all times we keep in mind that because the presumption is that the responding party pays for discovery requests, the burden remains with CBRE to demonstrate that costs should be shifted to Plaintiffs. *See Zubulake (III)*, 216 F.R.D. at 283." *Id.* at 573.

[2] The case involved a claim of defective design or manufacture of a tire. Plaintiff sought discovery related to the general failure of Cooper's tires, "with no restriction on the manner or reason for that failure." 2007 Ala. LEXIS 229, at *35. On a writ of mandamus, the Alabama Supreme Court said that this was too broad. "[T]he trial court exceeded its discretion in

In considering whether the discovery of ESI is unduly burdensome, the trial court may consider the application of computer search and retrieval programs[3] that enable useful information to be obtained rapidly and effectively. In the context of electronic-information management, a litany of the amount of information to be disclosed by page or the amount of work to be expended if a person was to handle each such page individually is not a persuasive argument for showing that the trial court in this case exceeded its discretion. However, we recognize that Cooper has presented evidence in the form of an affidavit that its burden of production with respect to e-mails will entail thousands of hours and will cost hundreds of thousands of dollars. In light of this showing by Cooper, we believe that it is appropriate for the trial court to consider in more detail Cooper's arguments as to its cost of producing e-mails. In making its determination as to the proper extent of discovery of Cooper's relevant ESI, including e-mails, the trial court should consider the recent changes to the Federal Rules of Civil Procedure. See, e.g., R. Noel Clinard and William M. Ragland, *A Practical Guide to E-Discovery Amendments to the Federal Rules of Civil Procedure* (Eleventh Circuit Judicial Conference, May 2007). Of particular importance will be a consideration of the extent to which the ESI ordered produced is accessible under the new guidelines set out by the changes to Federal Rules of Civil Procedure 16, 26, 33, 34, 37, and 45 and Form 35. Also relevant, of course, will be the extent to which the material in question has already been produced.

Id. at *37–39. The court then described the analysis in *Wiginton* and concluded that "the consideration of factors analogous to those applied in *Wiginton* would be an appropriate exercise of the trial court's discretion in considering the extent to which Cooper should comply with the plaintiffs' discovery request for ESI." *Id.* at *44.

In *Analog Devices, Inc. v. Michalski*, 2006 NCBC LEXIS 16 (N.C. Super. Ct. Nov. 1, 2006), the superior court determined that North Carolina's rules of procedure should govern a cost-shifting analysis with respect to

---

holding that the plaintiffs are entitled to discovery of information regarding the failures of all tires manufactured by Cooper, even those unrelated to tread separation, and the trial court is directed to limit its discovery order accordingly." *Id.* at 36. The court held instead that "the plaintiffs' discovery might appropriately be limited to those Cooper tires manufactured from the same or substantially similar 'skim stock' rubber using the same or similar manufacturing processes." *Id.* at 35–36.

[3] The Alabama Supreme Court did not further identify these "programs."

the costs of restoring e-mails from backup tapes. The court applied N.C. R. Civ. P. 26(b)(1) to determine if the cost of producing e-mails on the backup tapes was unduly burdensome in light of their probative value. *Id.* at *47. The court considered five factors in its analysis: "(1) the burden and expense of production; (2) the needs of the case; (3) the amount in controversy; (4) any limitations on the parties' resources; and (5) the importance of the issues at stake." *Id.* The court held that "[t]he uncertainty of the cost combined with the potential probative value of the discovery is too great to deny Defendants' motion." *Id.* at *54. This was a misappropriation of trade secrets case, and the court also recognized the importance of the issues at stake impacting the state's public interest in permitting employees to move freely with an employer's interest in protecting its trade secrets. *Id.* at *52. Furthermore, the court found that the costs involved would not be outcome determinative. *Id.* at *54. Ultimately, the court found that "[n]either party's ability to pursue its litigation goals will be impacted by cost-sharing." Therefore the court determined that each side should pay equally for the costs of restoration and recovery, while reserving the right to amend this ruling after the close of discovery. *Id.* at *55.

Mississippi has actually had a cost-shifting rule in place since 2003. Rule 26(a)(5) of Mississippi's civil rules provides:

> (5) Electronic Data. To obtain discovery of data or information that exists in electronic or magnetic form, the requesting party must specifically request production of electronic or magnetic data and specify the form in which the requesting party wants it produced. The responding party must produce the electronic or magnetic data that is responsive to the request and is reasonably available to the responding party in its ordinary course of business. If the responding party cannot-through reasonable efforts-retrieve the data or information requested or produce it in the form requested, the responding party must state an objection complying with these rules. If the court orders the responding party to comply with the request, the court may also order that the requesting party pay the reasonable expenses of any extraordinary steps required to retrieve and produce the information.[4]

---

[4] See www.fjc.gov/public/pdf.nsf/lookup/ElecDi11.pdf/$file/ElecDi11.pdf. Connecticut also permits cost-shifting. See Superior Court Civil Rules, Sec. 13-9(d) (available in the 2008 Connecticut Practice Book at www.jud.ct.gov/Publications/PracticeBook/pb1.pdf): "(d) If data has been electronically stored, the judicial authority may for good cause shown

New Hampshire, New York, and North Carolina are states that have meet and confer requirements that require discussion of discovery issues associated with electronically stored information.[5] New Hampshire's meet and confer session precedes the "structuring conference" required

---

order disclosure of the data in an alternative format provided the data is otherwise discoverable. When the judicial authority considers a request for a particular format, the judicial authority may consider the cost of preparing the disclosure in the requested format and may enter an order that one or more parties shall pay the cost of preparing the disclosure." As *Analog Devices* and the Mississippi and Connecticut rules reflect, cost-shifting may be handled differently in the states. *See, e.g.,* Texas Rule 196.4 (If a responding party cannot through reasonable efforts retrieve electronic data or information requested or produce it in the form requested, the responding party must state an objection. If the court then orders the responding party to comply with the request, the court must also order that the requesting party pay the reasonable expenses of any extraordinary steps required to retrieve and produce the information). California Code Section 2031.280(b) provides that a *requesting party* should pay the costs of translating data compilations into reasonably usable forms: "(b) If necessary, the responding party at the reasonable expense of the demanding party shall, through detection devices, translate any data compilations included in the demand into reasonably usable form." *Toshiba America Electronics Components, Inc. v. Superior Court,* 124 Cal. App. 4th 762 (2004) (requiring the requesting party to pay the costs of restoration of information on 800 backup tapes, which was estimated to be $1.9 million, but allowing a motion for a protective order to be filed if the requesting party disputes the necessity or reasonableness of the expenses sought by the producing party). In New York, a number of cases have addressed the issue. *Lipco Electrical Corp. et al. v. ASG Consulting Corp. et al.,* 2004 NY Misc. LEXIS 1337 (N.Y. Sup. Ct. Aug. 18, 2004) ("However, cost shifting of electronic discovery is not an issue in New York since the courts have held that, under the CPLR, the party seeking discovery should incur the costs incurred in the production of discovery material. (Citation omitted.) CPLR 3103(a) specifically grants the court authority to issue a protective order to prevent a party from incurring unreasonable expenses in complying with discovery demands. Therefore, the analysis of whether electronic discovery should be permitted in New York is much simpler than it is in the federal courts. The court need only determine whether the material is discoverable and whether the party seeking the discovery is willing to bear the cost of production of the electronic material. This is especially true in this case where Lipco/Action has been provided with hard copies of the electronically stored data."); *Etzion v. Etzion,* 2005 MY Misc. LEXIS 519 (N.Y. Sup. Ct., Feb. 17, 2005 (citations omitted) ("Plaintiff requested that defendant provide her with the sum of $ 15,000 for her attorney and an equal amount, $ 15,000, for her computer expert. Under the CPLR, the party seeking discovery should incur the costs in the production of discovery material." "The court therefore determines that plaintiff shall bear the cost of the production of the business records she seeks, subject to any possible reallocation of costs at trial."); *Delta Financial Corp. et al. v. Morrison et al.,* 2006 NY Misc. LEXIS 2232 (Sup. Ct. N.Y., Aug. 17, 2006) (ordering a sampling of backup tapes to be restored and initially requiring the requesting party initially to pay 100 percent of the costs of "restoration, deduplication processes and attorneys' fees and costs with regard to the review of the documents for privilege.")
[5] Utah also has a meet and confer requirement that mimics Fed.R.Civ.P. 26(f). See Utah Rule 26(f) at www.utcourts.gov/resources/rules/urcp/.

under New Hampshire's Superior Court rules. Under Rule 62.(I)(C) of these rules,[6] at the meet and confer session, the parties are required to discuss "(4) the scope of discovery, including particularly with respect to information stored electronically or in any other medium, the extent to which such information is reasonably accessible, the likely costs of obtaining access to such information and who shall bear said costs, the form in which such information is to be produced, the need for and the extent of any holds or other mechanisms that have been or should be put in place to prevent the destruction of such information, and the manner in which the parties propose to guard against the waiver of privilege claims with respect to such information."

New York's meet and confer obligation appears in Section 202.70 of New York's Uniform Rules for the Supreme Court and County Court which contains the Rules of the Commercial Division of the Supreme Court.[7] Subsection (g) contains the rules of practice for the Commercial Division and Rule 8 is entitled, "Consultation prior to Preliminary and Compliance Conferences." It provides that counsel shall consult prior to a preliminary or compliance conference with the court about, *inter alia,* discovery issues and in particular states: "(b) Prior to the preliminary conference, counsel shall confer with regard to anticipated electronic discovery issues. Such issues shall be addressed with the court at the preliminary conference and shall include but not be limited to (i) implementation of a data preservation plan; (ii) identification of relevant data; (iii) the scope, extent and form of production; (iv) anticipated cost of data recovery and proposed initial allocation of such cost; (v) disclosure of the programs and manner in which the data is maintained; (vi) identification of computer system(s) utilized; (vii) identification of the individual(s) responsible for data preservation; (viii) confidentiality and privilege issues; and (ix) designation of experts."

North Carolina has local rules for its Business Courts which contain a meet and confer requirement prior to a case management meeting with the court.[8] Under Rule 17.1, the parties are required to cover these issues: "(i) An estimate of the volume of documents and/or electronic information likely to be the subject of discovery in the case from parties and nonparties and whether there are technological means, including but not limited to production of electronic images rather than paper documents

---

[6] See www.nh.gov/judiciary/rules/sror/sror-h3-62.htm.

[7] See www.courts.state.ny.us/rules/trialcourts/202.shtml#70.

[8] See www.ncbusinesscourt.net/New/localrules/NCBC%20Amended%20Local%20Rules %20-%202006.doc.

and any associated protocol, that may render document discovery more manageable at an acceptable cost;" "(r) The need for retention of potentially relevant documents, including but not limited to documents stored electronically and the need to suspend all automatic deletions of electronic documents or overwriting of backup tapes which may contain potentially relevant information. The parties shall also discuss the need for a document preservation order;" "(s)The need for cost-shifting of expenses related to discovery of information stored electronically, including the restoration of back-up tapes and forensic examination of computers, and the possibility of obtaining the desired information from alternate sources at reduced expense;" "(t) The format in which the electronic records are to be produced, and procedures to avoid unnecessary burden and expense associated with such production. If metadata is to be produced, the parties shall discuss a protocol for producing such information, including the format for production (e.g., native, copy, original), and the ability to search such information;" and "(u) The need for security measures to be adopted to protect any information that is produced in electronic format or that will be converted into electronic format and stored on counsel's computer systems. Such discussion should encompass whether and under what circumstances clients will be afforded access to the information produced by another party and what security measures should be used for such access."[9]

The Conference of Chief Judges of the state courts has issued a set of guidelines on electronic discovery that closely follows the federal rules, *Guidelines for State Trial Courts Regarding Discovery of Electronically-Stored Information* (August 2006).[10]

Although most states do not require a conference among lawyers (Rule 26(f)) followed by a scheduling conference with the court (Rule 16) as is required under the federal rules, the guidelines suggest that in appropriate cases, state courts become more proactive on e-discovery issues. For example, Guideline 2 explains when a court should encourage counsel to

---

[9] North Carolina's business court rules also cover cost-shifting. Rule 18.6(b) provides, "Prior to filing motions and objections relating to discovery of information stored electronically, the parties shall discuss the possibility of shifting costs for electronic discovery, the use of Rule 30(b)(6) depositions of information technology personnel, and informal means of resolving disputes regarding technology and electronically stored information. The certificate required by Rule 18.6(a) shall address efforts to resolve the dispute through these and any other means related to discovery of information stored."

[10] It can be found at www.ncsconline.org/WC/Publications/CS_ElDiscCCJGuidelines.pdf.

become informed about his or her client's "relevant" information management systems:

> In any case in which an issue regarding the discovery of electroni-
> cally-stored information is raised or is likely to be raised, a judge
> should, when appropriate, encourage counsel to become familiar
> with the operation of the party's relevant information manage-
> ment systems, including how information is stored and retrieved.
> If a party intends to seek the production of electronically-stored
> information in a specific case, that fact should be communicated to
> opposing counsel as soon as possible and the categories or types of
> information to be sought should be clearly identified.

Guideline 3 then provides that judges should "encourage" lawyers
to meet and confer to "voluntarily come to agreement on the electronically stored information to be disclosed, the manner of its disclosure, and
a schedule that will enable discovery to be completed within the time
period specified by [the Rules of Procedure or the scheduling order]."

Guideline 4 then recommends that the court hold a hearing to address
the results of the lawyers' "meet and confer session":

> Following the exchange of the information specified in Guideline
> 3, or a specially set hearing, or a mandatory conference early in
> the discovery period, a judge should inquire whether counsel have
> reached agreement on any of the following matters and address
> any disputes regarding these or other electronic discovery issues:
> A. The electronically-stored information to be exchanged includ-
> ing information that is not readily accessible;
> B. The form of production;
> C. The steps the parties will take to segregate and preserve rel-
> evant electronically stored information;
> D. The procedures to be used if privileged electronically-stored
> information is inadvertently disclosed; and
> E. The allocation of costs.

The remaining six guidelines address the scope of e-discovery, form
of production,[11] reallocation of costs, inadvertent disclosure of privileged

---

[11] Effective May 1, 2008, Idaho amended its version of F.R.Civ.P. 34 to include electronically
stored information and to provide for sampling of such information. See www.isc.idaho.
gov/rules/ircp34.rul. Illinois Supreme Court Rule 201 addresses the scope of discovery and
defines documents to include "all retrievable information in computer storage." See www.
state.il.us/court/SupremeCourt/Rules/Art_II/ArtII.htm#201. Illinois Rule 214 allows a

information, preservation orders, and sanctions and, for the most part, appear to parallel the federal rules.

A number of states have now modified their rules of civil procedures to address many of these issues.[12]

Eventually, there will be a convergence of standards in federal and state courts that, except perhaps with respect to cost-shifting, will start to look alike.

---

party to make a written request to inspect or sample documents and, unless objection is made, "A party served with the written request shall (1) produce the requested documents as they are kept in the usual course of business or organized and labeled to correspond with the categories in the request, and all retrievable information in computer storage in printed form." See www.state.il.us/court/SupremeCourt/Rules/Art_II/ArtII.htm#214.

[12] In the period 2006–2008, several states now have adopted some or all of the e-discovery components of the federal rules verbatim or with very similar language. See Arizona (www.supreme.state.az.us/rules/ramd_pdf/r-06-0034.pdf); Indiana (www.in.gov/judiciary/orders/rule-amendments/2007/trial-091007.pdf); Iowa (www.judicial.state.ia.us/wfdata/frame6744-1671/File58.pdf contains the Supreme Court's order and www.legis.state.ia.us/Rules/Current/court/courtrules.pdf contains the text of Iowa Court Rules); Louisiana (www.legis.state.la.us/billdata/streamdocument.asp?did=447007 contains Act No. 140 which amends CCP 1424 (www.legis.state.la.us/lss/lss.asp?doc=111195) showing the changes in CCP1460 (www.legis.state.la.us/lss/lss.asp?doc=111233), CCP1461 (www.legis.state.la.us/lss/lss.asp?doc=111234), and CCP 1462 (www.legis.state.la.us/lss/lss.asp?doc=111235); Maryland (www.courts.state.md.us/rules/rodocs/ro158.pdf); Minnesota (www.mncourts.gov/documents/0/Public/NewsPostings/Public_Notice_07/ORADM048001-0521.pdf); Montana (See Montana Code Annotated (Rules of Civil Procedure) for Rules 16, 26, 33, 34, 37 and 45 available at data.opi.state.mt.us/bills/mca_toc/25_20.htm); Nebraska (www.supremecourt.ne.gov/rules/amendments/DiscoveryAmds.pdf); New Jersey (See Rule 1:9 addressing subpoenas at www.judiciary.state.nj.us/rules/part-1toc.htm and Rules 4:5B, 4:10, 4:17, 4:18, 4:23-6, addressing case management conferences, the scope of discovery, interrogatories, production of documents, and sanctions at www.judiciary.state.nj.us/rules/part4toc.htm); and Utah (see Rules 26, 33, 34, and 37 in the Utah Rules of Civil Procedure at www.utcourts.gov/resources/rules/urcp/).

CHAPTER TWENTY-ONE

Conclusion

There are a number of "takeaways" from these e-discovery cases. They include the following:

- Communication with the client, among counsel, and with the court is critical.
- Vendors can get a party in to e-discovery trouble; choose wisely and supervise closely.
- Between fishing expeditions and smoking guns are "tilt" documents that will determine if discovery on discovery is allowed.
- The prelitigation duty to preserve continues to be a major worry in a world where electronic information can disappear rapidly.
- Agreement on keywords for searches which can be fairly reached among counsel will avoid numerous problems later.
- The concept of "reasonably usable form" may dictate who wins "form of production" arguments.
- Rapid movement of data to backup tapes is the subject of growing concern in the case law.
- Don't make representations in court that can't be backed up.
- *Zubulake*'s statement of counsel's discovery responsibilities is becoming a standard.
- There are a number of avenues to sanctions under the Federal Rules of Civil Procedure.
- Beware of electronic discovery of experts by subpoena.
- Subpoena recipients can be expected to make a case of undue burden and cost when faced with nontailored requests for electronically stored information.

Add your own to this list, but remember the three guideposts that must be followed if e-discovery is going to work:

1. E-discovery decisions should always be based on honoring the goal of Rule 1 of the Federal Rules of Civil Procedure: the just, speedy, and inexpensive determination of every action.
2. The rule of reason should control e-discovery decision making.
3. Judges must become involved in the e-discovery process to protect the levelness of the playing field, to ensure that Rule 1 is satisfied, and to affirm reasonable e-discovery behavior.

INDEX

ABOUT THE AUTHOR

John M. Barkett

Mr. Barkett is a partner at the law firm of Shook, Hardy & Bacon L.L.P., in its Miami office. He is a graduate of the University of Notre Dame (B.A. Government, 1972, *summa cum laude*) and the Yale Law School (J.D. 1975) and served as a law clerk to the Honorable David W. Dyer on the old Fifth Circuit Court of Appeals. Mr. Barkett has been an adjunct professor of law at the University of Miami Law School for the past five years.

Mr. Barkett has, over the years, been a commercial litigator (contract and corporate disputes, employment, trademark, and antitrust), environmental litigator (CERCLA, RCRA, and toxic tort), and, for the past several years, a peacemaker and problem solver, serving as an arbitrator, mediator, facilitator, or allocator in a variety of environmental or commercial contexts. He is a certified mediator under the rules of the Supreme Court of Florida, serves on the CPR Institute for Dispute Resolution's "Panel of Distinguished Neutrals," and is on National Roster of Environmental Dispute Resolution and Consensus Building Professionals maintained by the U.S. Institute for Environmental Conflict Resolution. He has served or is serving as a neutral in more than fifty matters involving in the aggregate more than $450 million. In November 2003, he was appointed by the presiding judge to serve as the special master to oversee the implementation and enforcement of the 1992 consent decree between the United States and the State of Florida relating to the restoration of the Florida Everglades. He also consults with major corporations on the evaluation of legal strategy and risk and conducts independent investigations where such services are needed.

Mr. Barkett serves on the Council of the ABA Section of Litigation after service as the section's codirector of CLE and cochair of the Environmental Litigation Committee. He is the author of numerous works in the e-discovery arena including:

- *Bytes, Bits and Bucks: Cost-Shifting and Sanctions in E-Discovery*, ABA Section of Litigation Annual Meeting (2004) and 71 Def. Couns. J. 334 (2004)
- *The Prelitigation Duty to Preserve: Lookout!*, ABA Annual Meeting, Chicago (2005)
- *Help Is On The Way ... Sort Of: How the Civil Rules Advisory Committee Hopes to Fill the E-Discovery Void*, ABA Section of Litigation Annual Meeting, Los Angeles (2006)

- *Help Has Arrived... Sort Of: The New E-Discovery Rules*, ABA Section of Litigation Annual Meeting, San Antonio (2007)
- *The Battle for Bytes: New Rule 26*, e-Discovery (ABA Section of Litigation February 2006)
- *The Pieces to the Privilege Protection Puzzle*, 22 N.R.E 50 (2007)
- *E-Discovery For Arbitrators*, 1 Dis. Res. Int. J. 129 (Dec. 2007)
- *The Ethics of E-Discovery* (soon to be published by the American Bar Association).

In the fall of 2007, Mr. Barkett taught a first-ever course at the University of Miami Law School entitled "E-Discovery."

Mr. Barkett is editor and one of the authors of the Section of Litigation's Monograph, *Ex Parte Contacts with Former Employees* (Environmental Litigation Committee October 2002). His paper, *A Baker's Dozen: Reasons Why You Should Read the 2002 Model Rules of Professional Conduct*, was presented at the Section of Litigation's 2003 Annual Conference. Mr. Barkett also wrote *The MJP Maze: Avoiding the Unauthorized Practice of Law*, which was presented at the 2005 Section of Litigation Annual Conference. He also wrote *Refresher Ethics: Conflicts of Interest*, for the section's January 2007 Joint Environmental, Products Liability, and Mass Torts CLE program and *Tattletales or Crimestoppers: Disclosure Ethics under Model Rules 1.6 and 1.13*, presented at the ABA Annual Meeting (Atlanta, August 7, 2004), and, in an updated version, at the ABA Tort and Insurance Practice Section Spring CLE Meeting (Phoenix, April 11, 2008). Mr. Barkett also presented his paper, *From Canons to Cannon* at the Ethics Centennial sponsored by the ABA Section of Litigation (Washington, D.C., April 18, 2008) Commemorating the one hundredth anniversary of the adoption of the Canons of Ethics.

Mr. Barkett is also the author of *Ethical Issues in Environmental Dispute Resolution*, a chapter in the ABA publication, *Environmental Dispute Resolution, An Anthology of Practical Experience* (July 2002); *The Courtroom of the Twenty-First Century—ADR, Conflict Management* (ADR Committee, ABA Section of Litigation Summer 2002); *The Pieces to the Privilege Protection Puzzle*, 22 N.R.E. 50 (2007); and *Tipping the Scales of Justice: The Ride of* ADR, 22 NRE 40 (Spring 2008).

Among his other works are a terrorism-related article on torts, entitled, *If Terror Reigns, Will Torts Follow?* 9 Widener Law Symposium 485 (2003); *A Database Analysis of the Superfund Allocation Case Law*, Shook, Hardy & Bacon L.L.P. (Miami 2003); and *The CERCLA Limitations Puzzle*, 19 N.R.E. 70 (2004).

Mr. Barkett has recently been recognized in the areas of alternative dispute resolution and environmental law in a number of lawyer-recognition publications, including Who's Who Legal (International Bar Association) (since 2005); Best Lawyers in America (National Law Journal) (since 2005); Legal Elite (since 2004) (Florida Trend); and Chambers USA America's Leading Lawyers (since 2004). Mr. Barkett can be reached at jbarkett@shb.com.

2008 WL 66932